Creating Romantic Purses

Creating Romantic Purses

Patterns &
Instructions
for Unique
Handbags

Marilyn Green
Carole Cree

STERLING/CHAPELLE
An imprint of Sterling Publishing Co., Inc.

New York / London
www.sterlingpublishing.com

Chapelle, Ltd., Inc., P.O. Box 9252, Ogden, UT 84409
    (801) 621-2777 • (801) 621-2788 Fax
    e-mail: chapelle@chapelleltd.com
    Web site: www.chapelleltd.com

The copy, photographs, instructions, illustrations, and designs in
this volume are intended for the personal use of the reader and may be
reproduced for that purpose only. Any other use, especially commercial use, is
forbidden under law without the written permission of the copy-right holder.
    Every effort has been made to ensure that all information in this book is
accurate. However, due to differing conditions, tools, and individual skills, the
publisher cannot be responsible for any injuries, losses, and/or other damages
which may result from the use of the information in this book.
    Due to limited amount of available space, we must print our patterns at a
reduced size in order to give our patrons the maximum number
of patterns possible in our publications. We believe the quality and quantity of
our patterns will compensate for any inconvenience this may cause.
    This volume is meant to stimulate craft ideas. If readers are un-familiar or not
proficient in a skill necessary to attempt a project, we urge that they refer to an
instructional book specifically addressing the required technique.

STERLING and the distinctive Sterling logo are registered trademarks of
Sterling Publishing Co., Inc.

Library of Congress Cataloging-in-Publication Data

Green, Marilyn V.   646.48 GRE
  Creating romantic purses : patterns & instructions for unique handbags /
Marilyn Green & Carole Cree.
      p. cm.
  "A Sterling/Chapelle Book."
  Includes index.
  ISBN-13: 978-1-4027-2517-3
  ISBN-10: 1-4027-2517-5
  1. Handbags. I. Cree, Carole. II. Title.

TT667.G74 2006
646.4'8--dc22
                                                    2005027881

10 9 8 7 6 5 4 3 2 1

Published by Sterling Publishing Co., Inc.
387 Park Avenue South, New York, NY 10016
©2006 Marilyn Green and Carole Cree
Distributed in Canada by Sterling Publishing
c/o Canadian Manda Group, 165 Dufferin Street
Toronto, Ontario, Canada M6K 3H6
Distributed in the United Kingdom by GMC Distribution Services,
Castle Place, 166 High Street, Lewes, East Sussex, England BN7 1XU
Distributed in Australia by Capricorn Link (Australia) Pty. Ltd.
P.O. Box 704, Windsor, NSW 2756, Australia

Printed and Bound in China
All Rights Reserved

Sterling ISBN-13: 978-1-4027-2517-3 (hardcover)
        ISBN-10: 1-4027-2517-5

Sterling ISBN-13: 978-1-4027-5370-1 (paperback)
        ISBN-10: 1-4027-5370-5

For information about custom editions, special sales, premium
and corporate purchases, please contact Sterling Special Sales
Department at 800-805-5489 or specialsales@sterlingpublishing.com.

Table of Contents

Chapter 1

Where the Romance Begins

Sometimes it's love at first sight. Sometimes it's a slow fall. A piece of old glowing velvet catches your eye at a flea market and you simply must have it—you're not certain why. At a garage sale, you find some irresistible old buttons and a length of beautiful vintage ribbon, still in good condition. Later, you buy a piece of antique lace—fanciful and mysterious. After a few more purchases, dictated by a growing idea, you see that these things look even more interesting arranged together. You realize you have the makings of a one-of-a-kind purse, very much like the ones you have so admired. You are in love and the romance has begun.

Whatever the goal, the search for just the right pieces and parts, just the right blending of color and shade, just the right texture and touch, should be approached with a sense of adventure. After all, it encourages us to venture into places perhaps long forgotten among our own belongings; or even better, it gives us a reason to explore the endless corridors of antique stores, flea markets, tag sales, yard sales, and garage sales.

Fabrics

First select the material to be used as the body of the purse, as all other choices will be based around this basic color scheme and texture. One of the most obvious choices for a romantic purse is a vintage crazy quilt. The variety of fabrics, velvets, silks, and satins interspersed with ribbons, hand-painting, and decorative stitching inspires a romantic vision.

As we admire the wonderful handwork present on all vintage crazy quilts, we do not suggest that you cut into a preserved quilt. With a bit of diligent shopping, it is possible to find odd crazy-quilt squares here and there; or a *cutter* quilt, which is mostly unsalvageable but may have enough strong, intact areas to serve as the body of a romantic purse. The integrity of the fabric is a most important consideration. It is necessary to choose a piece that can stand up to a bit of tugging and testing. A purse, by its nature, suffers much handling and should be up to the task. A small worn spot should not be viewed as reason for rejection as it presents a perfect place to apply a bit of lace, ribbon, embroidery, or even a button or brooch.

If a crazy quilt is not your choice, there are a myriad of other choices. Flea markets and attics are full of vintage fabrics. Old drapery panels,

folded for years in a forgotten box, upholstery fabric from long ago, or dress fabric never used.

There is something about the passing years that gives these older textiles a soft muted look and feel that a new fabric does not possess. Choose a fabric with a subtle pattern—one that is not so large that it will be lost when cut—and a soft muted blend of color. Think of how the purse is to be used. Choose a color or combination of colors that will allow the owner to carry the purse often.

The perfect romantic purse begins with the choices of fabrics, trims, and embellishments. There are many ways to approach these choices. The decision begins with whether we see the purse as a compilation of items that evoke memories or a as statement of our personal artistic views.

Another fabric choice certain to create a romantic mood is vintage lace. Lace is readily available in most antique shops or flea markets. Construct the base of the purse from a new fabric, perhaps an ivory moiré or silk, then cover the body with a collage of lace pieces. Layering laces gives a rich texture, and the blending of the various shades of aged lace creates a soft combination of shades from ivory to deep ecru. Layering also allows the use of some pieces that may be a bit worn. In effect, we are creating a patchwork of lace, a bit reminiscent of the Normandy lacework so popular around the turn of the twentieth century.

Consider the choice of a new fabric. Since our focus is romance, there are several new fabrics that spring to mind. One we enjoy using is silk. The choices are sumptuous, elegant, and extravagant. As you journey through the book, you will see that we have chosen several silks that have been overshot with embroidery. Most of our selections offer floral designs with trailing vines interspersed with softly shaded blossoms. Once again, color is a consideration, keeping in mind that when it comes time to select trims and embellishments you will want to draw from the colors displayed in the pattern or embroidery.

A silk fabric will dictate that these trims and embellishments be more delicate in nature than those used on heavier, more-textured fabrics.

Another fabric to be considered is trimmed chenille. A light upholstery-weight chenille fabric is an excellent choice for the body of a purse. We do not recommend an upholstery fabric with a heavy, stiff backing. This will make the fabric too heavy for a purse. Choose a fabric with a small pattern, perhaps in the case of chenille, a small polka dot or floral design.

Another fabric we find irresistible in a romantic purse, is hand-dyed fabric. Heavy-weight fabrics with subtle patterns take on a romantic aura when they are washed with a combination of dye colors carefully selected to blend into a delightful hue.

Embellishments

Now the real fun begins—beginning the search for embellishments. A decision must be made regarding a general theme for your embellishment plan. If you do not have a clear idea of how you want your purse to look, a bit of research may be in order. A quick look through any number of romantic magazines or books may provide the inspiration you need. Be alert to groups of like objects that catch your imagination. A collection of these objects from which to choose is helpful when arranging

your collage. Cluster things together in like metals, such as all silvertone or all brasstone. Let the fabric talk to you—cooler colors like silver and warmer shades like brass. Be alert for a bright rhinestone pin or earring that may pick up a color in the embroidery or the print, or perhaps one in a contrasting color that will serve as an accent piece.

Crazy quilts offer the perfect background for vintage and antique objects. A readily available grouping of objects might be found in the button box. It is important to select buttons with a vintage flavor in keeping with the theme set by the quilt itself. The gently aged patina of old mother-of-pearl buttons is a wonderful choice. By selecting a grouping comprised of various sizes and shapes, and interspersing them with bits of antique lace, embroidered or beaded pieces, and arranging them to fit the angles created by the crazy patch itself, a pattern is certain to emerge. An important design element to keep in mind when creating your collage is to keep the grouping tight, overlapping materials and allowing the various parts of the design to touch one another.

Another choice to be used on the vintage-themed romantic purse are antique watch faces, hands, or dials. Couched ribbons or trailing silk embroidery with small groups of watch dials nestled in the handwork is another unique design idea.

A varied group of vintage brooches offers another obvious choice to bring romance to a crazy-quilt purse. Find brooches that blend in a certain colourway and add interest by varying in size and shape. The brooches can be interspersed with buttons and lace motifs.

If you are using a fabric, such as chenille, tapestry, or velvet, explore using floral pieces or old millinery materials. A "corsage" can be created by searching antique malls for velvet leaves, vintage stamens, blossoms, and petals. Keep the pieces in a central colourway and combine your treasures, using floral wire and perhaps a needle and thread. The component parts might be assembled using a lace hanky or a lace motif as the base, then attached to the flap or a lower corner of the purse.

Your embellishment collage or grouping will be the focal point of the romantic purse. Don't forget to save a button or two, a piece of ribbon, a small brooch or a stray lace motif to be used as an unexpected treat on the back of the bag.

Trims

Another important component is the choice of trimmings. Many purses are adorned with a most interesting trim we call looped fringe, constructed of rayon seam binding. This unique trimming adds a whimsical element. The finished fringe comes in two lengths, 1½" and 3". The rayon content allows the fringe to have a soft, draping appearance and if the color is carefully selected, can add a vintage flavor to the purse; just as a clear, more vibrant shade is perfect for a more contemporary look. Use a double row of fringe to give the area a full and lush look.

Another trim we use extensively is a flat braid made from the same rayon seam binding that is used to make the looped fringe. The braid, which is approximately ⅜" wide, has a braided center flanked by softly scalloped edges. It is perfect for covering the looped fringe

header and any unfinished edges that may need a bit of camouflaging.

Use other fringes, braids, cords, beads, and metallic threads. You will find an interesting assortment of trims in most high-end fabric shops or upscale home decorating shops. Do not forget to scour antique shops for elegant trims and braids.

Whether you keep and carry the purse or offer it as a precious gift, it is our hope that the journey to its completion will bring you hours of joy and the peace and contentment found in time well spent.

How to use this book

The projects in this book can either be made exactly as shown in the photograph, or altered to create a similar purse with your personality. Each titled purse gives a detailed list of materials and offers tips specific to making the purse shown. If you choose to alter the materials, refer to the generic list that accompanies the patterns for that purse in the Patterns Section. Use only one of the materials lists. However, no matter which materials list you choose, use the instructions and patterns given in the Pattern Section to construct the purse.

Crazy quilts are a history book of the Victorian era. It was a very sentimental time because Queen Victoria was so in love with Albert and adored her many children. Piecing and quilting were parlor pastimes for the well-to-do, using delicate fabrics left from fine dresses. They took great pride in their needlework and tried to outdo each other. One can see the stitcher's pleasure in these quilts. Perhaps you can't own a crazy quilt, but you can own one of these crazy-quilt purses and hold bits of history in your hand.

Victorian Vignette

The rich colors of this exquisite crazy quilt provide a lush background for an array of dazzling vintage pieces. Vintage brooches for sparkle, antique buttons, embroidered butterflies, and a lovely woman's portrait are layered perfectly by the artist. A stunning bag with which to dress up or down.

Materials
- Cotton cord, ½"-wide (2 yds) for rolled strap
- Crazy-quilt pieces: 10" x 7"; 17" x 11" (2)
- Fusible interfacing (¼ yd) for flap
- Fusible lightweight fleece (½ yd)
- Glues: fabric; industrial-strength
- Lining fabric (½ yd)
- Magnetic snap
- Rayon looped fringes, 2"-long: harvest gold (1 yd); soft mauve (2 yds)
- Velvet 3" x 30", cut on bias for rolled strap

Embellishments
- Embroidered butterflies (2)
- Hand-dyed ribbon, ¼"-wide for couching
- Silk print scrap
- Vintage beaded motif
- Vintage brooches (2)
- Vintage buttons (11)
- Vintage crocheted motifs (2)
- Vintage metallic trim, ¼"-wide (21")
- Vintage oval pin

Pattern and Instructions
Refer to Pattern 2 on pages 102–104. If you prefer to use different fabrics and trims than those listed above, use the generic list of materials listed with the pattern.

Vintage pin detail

Design Tips

❁ Sew fleece to pieces just outside the stitching line. If your quilt pieces are thick, you may prefer to fuse the fleece to the lining.

❁ Vintage crazy quilts are made of many fabrics and some will be more damaged than others. Cover these areas with pieces of lace or ribbon. "Age" these pieces by dipping in tea.

Joy Forever

The deep tone in this beautiful illustration of Victorian legacy reminds one of a fabulous piece of jewelry for all to admire. The art of beadwork is displayed and crowned with a porcelain pin. You remember what they say about a thing of beauty? It's a joy forever.

Materials
- Brown faux suede, 3" x 30"
- Crazy-quilt pieces: 8" x 12"; 15" sq. (2)
- Fusible interfacing (¼ yd) for flap
- Fusible lightweight fleece (⅔ yd)
- Glues: fabric; industrial-strength
- Harvest gold rayon looped fringe, ½"-wide (4⅛ yds)
- Lining fabric (⅔ yd)
- Magnetic snap
- Old gold grosgrain ribbon, 4"-wide (2 yds)

Embellishments
- Appliquéd brown velvet motif
- Brown chenille trim, ½"-wide (⅔ yd)
- Harvest gold flat trim, ½"-wide (2 yds)
- Tea-dyed flat lace trim, ½"-wide (2 yds)
- Vintage buttons (4)
- Vintage beaded motifs
- Vintage beads, assorted
- Vintage porcelain portrait brooch
- Vintage velvet beaded-bow appliqué

Pattern and Instructions
Refer to Pattern 20 on pages 139–141. If you prefer to use different fabrics and trims than those listed above, use the generic list of materials listed with the pattern.

Back view

Design Tips

❁ Stitch beads onto purse front. Apply glue with a toothpick to prevent beads from becoming loose.

❁ Sew two rows of looped fringe down sides and around bottom of purse front, and one row of fringe down sides and across bottom of back. Sew gusset to front. With right sides together, sew gusset to back. Turn right side out.

❁ Sew fleece to front and back just outside seam line. If crazy-quilt pieces are thick, fuse fleece to lining front and back.

❁ The bag strap is a 30" length of 4"-wide ribbon, a 3" x 30" piece of faux suede, and a 30" piece of harvest gold flat trim. Press in 1½" seam on each edge of ribbon, then proceed as instructed in the pattern. Center flat trim over grosgrain side of strap and sew in place. Use remaining ribbon for gusset.

❁ Crazy quilts are made of many fabrics; some fabrics wear quicker than others. Cover worn areas with bits of lace or ribbon. "Antique" these with tea dye.

Grandfather's Clock

Charming and witty, this bag reflects time past and present. The purse flap is covered with old typewriter keys, a clutch of antique watch faces, vintage buttons, and beads. The unusual color scheme and the spoke design on the quilt piece used for the body sets this purse apart from all the rest.

Materials
- Brown faux suede, 3" x 30" for strap
- Crazy-quilt pieces, 3" x 30" for strap; 8" x 12"
- Fusible interfacing (¼ yd) for flap
- Glues: fabric; industrial-strength
- Harvest gold looped fringe (3½ yds)
- Lightweight fusible fleece (⅔ yd)
- Magnetic snap
- Red looped fringe, ½"-wide (1⅔ yds)
- Scraps to piece, 15" sq. (2)
- Silk lining fabric (⅔ yd)

Embellishments
- Assorted rhinestones from old jewelry
- Black flat trim (⅔ yd)
- Embroidered vintage red ribbon, ¼"-wide (⅔ yd)
- Flower trim with ribbon
- Vintage buttons and beads
- Vintage flower parts for corsage
- Vintage typewriter keys
- Vintage watch and watch faces

Pattern and Instructions
Refer to Pattern 4 on pages 107–108. If you prefer to use different fabrics and trims than those listed above, use the generic list of materials listed with the pattern.

Back view

Design Tips

✿ This bag has three rows of looped fringe around the sides and bottom of the bag. Place a row of red between two rows of harvest gold, and two rows of looped fringe around the flap with harvest gold on top and red on bottom.

✿ When applying collected embellishment items to your bag, use fabric glue and/or hand-stitch fabric trims. Use industrial-strength glue for solid items such as watch parts, broken jewelry, and buttons.

✿ Add extra interest with a theme in your embellishments. The typewriter keys spell "PAST TIME" and the watch and watch parts all follow in the same theme of "Time."

Family Album

What a sweetheart—an absolute valentine! This purse is an album of family photographs and remnants of grandmother's fine dresses. It also holds a secret, so look closely. Can you see the crazy quilt is not old, but made from pieces of fabric you see in other purses in this book?

Materials
- Burgundy faux suede, 3" x 31" for strap
- Burgundy looped fringe (1 yd)
- Burgundy/black polka dot silk lining fabric (½ yd)
- Cotton lightweight muslin (½ yd)
- Fabric of choice (¼ yd) for heart on bag back
- Fusible fleece (½ yd)
- Fusible interfacing (⅓ yd) for flap
- Narrow trims to cover seams:
  blue/green silk flower trim, ½"-wide (30")
  blue silk ruffle trim, ½"-wide (1¼ yds)
  grosgrain pansy trim (⅓ yd)
  multicolored silk flower trim, ½"-wide (⅔ yd)
  multicolored silk trim ½"-wide (⅓ yd)
  purple/green flower trim, ½"-wide (⅓ yd)
- Sage green flat trim, ½"-wide (31") for strap
- Sage looped fringe (1 yd)
- Velvet or silk fabric pieces 3" x 9" (12 different)

Embellishments
- Beaded velvet trim for frames, ¼"-wide (15")
- Embroidered flowers (4)
- Old pearls or beads for frames
- Silk vintage prints (2)

Pattern and Instructions

Refer to Pattern 5 on pages 109–110. If you prefer to use different fabrics and trims than those listed above, use the generic list of materials listed with the pattern.

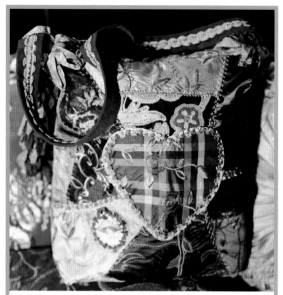

Back view

Design Tips

❀ Select fabrics in colors that are complementary to each other, and one color as the accent as with the pale blue.

❀ Cut 2–3 pattern pieces from each fabric.

❀ Use some of the silk lining fabric in the crazy-quilt design. *Note: This adds interest when you open the bag.*

❀ Cover some seams with hand- or machine-embroidery stitching, then cover some with the narrow trims.

❀ Make the heart piece for the back of the bag according to pattern instructions. Set aside.

❀ Randomly use old pearls and accent beads in the narrow trims used as frames around the silk prints and other accent pieces.

One Perfect Pouch

A perfect small handbag of beauty and mystery made from a fine bit of crazy quilt. The feathery trim covers like a veil but does not hide the amber-colored beads or the antique Bakelite buttons.

Materials
- Amber drop-bead fringe, ½"-wide (⅓ yd)
- Brown grosgrain ribbon, 1"-wide (1½ yds)
- Contrasting fabric, 6" x 9" for flap
- Eyelash fringe, 3"-wide (⅓ yd)
- Fusible fleece (¼ yd)
- Fusible interfacing (⅛ yd) for flap
- Glues: fabric; industrial-strength
- Magnetic snap
- Silk lining fabric (¼ yd)
- Vintage crazy-quilt pieces, 8" x 10" (2)
- Vintage metallic flat trim, ½"-wide (¾ yd)

Embellishments
- Assorted vintage buttons
- Lace leaves (4)
- Large vintage buttons (3)
- Vintage initial pins (2)
- Vintage lace scraps
- Vintage photo pin
- Vintage ribbon rose

Pattern and Instructions

Refer to Pattern 3 on pages 105–106. If you prefer to use different fabrics and trims than those listed above, use the generic list of materials listed with the pattern.

Back detail

Refer to Pattern 3 on pages 105–106.

Design Tips

❀ This small 8" x 7" x 2½" purse makes it easy to find nice vintage crazy-quilt pieces for the body of the bag. If a piece has a small flaw or two, simply place a piece of lace or ribbon embellishment over it with fabric glue.

❀ Use carefully selected new embellishments if you do not have access to vintage.

❀ The strap is constructed from two ¼ yard pieces of grosgrain sewn together close to the edge on both sides. The flat metallic trim is then placed in the center and stitched close to the edge of the trim on both sides. This makes a 26" strap. For a longer strap, increase the yardage of the ribbon and trim.

❀ Stitch drop-bead fringe inside flap and lining with right sides together. When flap is turned, bead drops dangle from edges. At this point, the eyelash trim can be stitched or glued with fabric glue to the edge of the flap.

❀ Stitch Bakelite buttons in the flap center and on the side seams where the strap is connected to the bag.

Timeless Classic

The large black silk bag, in timeless design and fabric, suits all your needs. But let's not be predictable or "Mercy me, dull." Add a little hum and buzz to show you are in touch with the times. All you need is a length of fabulous antique tapestry that adds just the right note and scale. The black flower is an unexpected high note and you will be singing a happy song when you find the small tapestry bag inside for coins or to use alone for small needs.

Materials

Large Purse
- Antique wool tapestry trim, 5"-wide (32")
- Black braid (4⅔ yds) for body and flap
- Black moiré (1⅔ yds) for lining
- Black silk with dots, 45"-wide (1⅔ yds)
- Fusible fleece (¾ yd)
- Fusible interfacing, 3" sq. (2)
- Large magnetic snap

Coin/Small Purse
- Antique wool tapestry trim, 5"-wide (13")
- Black moiré, 13" x 6" for lining
- Brass necklace fasteners (2)
- Fusible interfacing, 3" sq. (2)
- Gold tone chain for coin/small purse (38")
- Small magnetic snap

Embellishments
- Antique black buttons (2)
- Bar pins (2)
- Black felt circles, 2½"-dia. (2); 1½"-dia. (2)
- Black looped fringe, 3"-wide (⅔ yd)
- Glues: fabric; industrial-strength
- Handmade black rayon mums (2)
- Mums (2)

Continued on page 24

Design Tips

❁ The 5"-wide antique wool tapestry trim is stitched on back, front, and flap of the large purse.

❁ The chain strap on the small purse is detachable by using grommets. It is made from the antique wool tapestry and is lined with black moiré. *Note: If you plan to use it exclusively inside the larger bag, omit the mum and close with a loop around the black antique button.*

❁ Stitch edge of flat rayon trim to both sides of the wool tapestry trim and center on flap and around body of purse. Stitch flat rayon trim in the body seams just inside seam line, right sides facing. *Note: This gives the seam a scalloped finish.*

Timeless Classic *continued*

Pattern and Instructions

Finished size of large purse is 18½" x 12½" x 3". Finished size of coin purse is 5" square. Refer to Pattern 13 on pages 126–129. If you prefer to use different fabrics and trims than those listed on page 22, use the generic list of materials listed with the pattern.

Design Tips

✿ Construct a flat self-fabric strap according to the pattern.

✿ To make the mums, follow instructions in Pattern 15 on page 132.

Pansy Patch

"How do I love thee? Let me count the ways." I love your glowing jewel-like colors, your intriguing initials, and your rich chenille trim. I even love your back side with its unexpected surprises. But, most of all, I love your dear velvet pansies rescued from a hat bound for a most ignominious end.

Materials
- Antique buttons (3–4)
- Antique gold chain (1¼" yds)
- Beads, coordinating (9–10)
- Crazy-quilt pieces: 5" x 8"; 9" sq. (2)
- Curly fringe, 3"-wide (14")
- Fusible fleece (⅓ yd)
- Fusible interfacing (¼ yd) for flap
- Glues: fabric; industrial-strength
- Lining fabric (⅓ yd)
- Magnetic snap
- Vintage silk fringe, ½"-wide (14")

Embellishments
- Grosgrain ribbons, ⅜"-wide: olive green (¼ yd); purple (½ yd)
- Millinery pansies (4–5)
- Silk flower trim, ½"-wide (⅔ yd)
- Small brass heart charms (2)
- Vintage gold metallic embroidery with 4 motifs
- Vintage metallic embroidery with 4 motifs

Pattern and Instructions
Refer to Pattern 3 on pages 105–106. If you prefer to use different fabrics and trims than those listed above, use the generic list of materials listed with the pattern.

Design Tips

❀ With right side of flap up, sew curly fringe around flap edge. Fuse interfacing to flap cover, then sew lining to flap and turn. After bag is assembled, sew vintage silk fringe header. Hand-stitch silk flower trim on top of silk fringe. Stitch silk flower trim across back of bag or place trim where desired in crazy-quilt design.

❀ Glue pansies to bag front, covering weak or damaged areas.

❀ Make 3–5 ribbon flowers. Using purple ribbon, cut a 3" piece and fold end of ribbon down to make an angle at end. Gather-stitch from fold to the end of piece. Pull gathering thread to form a spiral. With folded end toward the middle, form a small flower, then stitch to secure.

❀ Make two accordion-folded pieces. Cut green ribbon in half and accordion-fold each, then stitch to secure. Stitch flowers and accordions around pansies before beads are strung and stitched.

❀ String 4–5 beads and stitch in the purple flower area; repeat on remaining side.

❀ Cut one motif from gold metallic piece. Glue three along front lower corner edge and one on opposite corner.

❀ Appliqué flowers on back. Center each flower with an antique button. *Note: You do not need flowers to use buttons; they make great embellishments almost anywhere on the bag.*

❀ Hand-stitch a chain with strong thread to bag at top of side seams. Stitch small brass heart charms to ends of chain.

Pansy Patch back view

The Softest Touch

Silk conjures romance, mystery and awe. It is wonderful how such beauty of nature is produced by way of a lowly silkworm.

The sumptuous silk bags cause us to imagine the caravans of camels and traders crossing the Arabian desert. We hear the trader haggling with a sheik about elegant silk hangings for his ordinary-looking tent. The inside of the tent soon glows with brilliant colors. The sheik drinks his tea seated on a thick cushion of silk with the softest touch, while basking in the beauty of romantic and mysterious silk.

Camelot

Purple and green don't work together!?! Au contraire! Imagine the finest Dutch iris with its purple blossom and green leaves. This silk bag is embroidered with more silk, 36 silver beads add shine, and a perfect green and purple beaded brooch is set at the clasp.

Materials
- Cotton cord, ½" dia. (2 yds) for rolled strap
- Fusible interfacing (¼ yd) for flap
- Fusible medium-weight fleece (½ yd)
- Glues: fabric; industrial-strength
- Lining fabric (½ yd)
- Magnetic snap
- Sage green rayon looped fringe, ½"-wide (4⅛ yds)
- Silk-embroidered purple silk (¾ yd)

Embellishments
- Flat trims: ½"-wide (⅔ yd each): purple, sage
- Porcelain brooch
- Purple eyelash trim (⅔ yd)

Pattern and Instructions
Refer to Pattern 2 on pages 102–104. If you prefer to use different fabrics and trims than those listed above, use the generic list of materials listed with the pattern.

Fringe detail

Refer to Pattern 2 on pages 102–104.

Design Tips

✿ Follow these steps to make flat trim, eyelash, and silver-bead trim.

1. Turn under one end of each of the two flat trims and the eyelash trim and stitch down.

2. Stack all three pieces, with eyelash on top.

3. Begin loosely braiding the three pieces, keeping right sides up and taking a securing stitch to hold in place while braiding.

4. When the braiding is long enough to fit along the edge of the purse flap, trim off any excess braid and finish ends by turning under and stitching.

5. Finish trim by stitching silver beads every inch or so along the length of the braided trim.

6. Set aside until you make the flap to be embellished.

✿ If you cannot find a suitable porcelain piece, a jeweled brooch or a silver pin will also do nicely.

Midnight Garden

Perhaps you have never encountered silk needle-point of such ravishing texture and color. The dark background makes the shades of pink, blue, and green almost pop out of your hand. The pearly buttons stitched onto the fringe are reminiscent of the manicured nails on the hand of a Chinese princess.

Materials
- Fusible interfacing (¼ yd) for flap
- Fusible medium-weight fleece (½ yd)
- Glues: fabric; industrial-strength
- Lining fabric (½ yd)
- Looped fringes, ½"-wide: cream (1 yd); sage green (2 yds)
- Magnetic snap
- Silk needlepoint fabric (¾ yd)

Embellishments
- Flat braid trim, ¼"-wide (¾ yd) for flat strap
- Flat sage braid trim, ¼"-wide (15") for flap
- Small vintage buttons (16)
- Stone donuts (2)

Pattern and Instructions
Refer to Pattern 1 on pages 99–101. If you prefer to use different fabrics and trims than those listed above, use the generic list of materials listed with the pattern.

Fringe detail

Design Tips

❋ Stitch small vintage buttons to the ends of the top layer of looped fringe around the purse flap.

❋ Embellish flat fabric strap by sewing flat braid trim down the center of the top of the strap.

❋ Attach the stone donuts by making a knot out of the flat strap trim, pulling the raw edges through the hole back, gluing securely with industrial-strength glue, then gluing to strap end at the seam.

❋ Place the sage flat braid along the edge of the flap and looped fringe.

Annie Oakley

Annie Oakley may not have had a silk bag sewn with turquoise stones or flighty feather trim, but given the chance, she would have thrown her lasso around this one. The brown embroidered silk has the look of leather from a distance, but in hand, the feel of a silk petticoat.

Materials

- Brown embroidered silk (¾ yd)
- Cotton piping, ½" dia. (2 yds) for rolled strap
- Fusible interfacing (¼ yd) for flap
- Fusible medium-weight fleece (½ yd)
- Glues: fabric; industrial-strength
- Lining fabric (½ yd)
- Looped fringe, 2¼"-wide (2 yds)

Embellishments

- Brown beaded stars (3)
- Flat braid trim, small (14")
- Flat turquoise stones (6)
- Sage green eyelash trim, 3"-wide (14")
- Small beads or brass rondels (6)
- Turquoise feather trim, 1½"-wide (14")

Pattern and Instructions

Refer to Pattern 1 on pages 99–101. If you prefer to use different fabrics and trims than those listed above, use the generic list of materials listed with the pattern.

Fringe detail

Design Tips

❀ If you cannot find embellishments as shown, use similar pieces that blend in color and are striking on the silk fabric chosen.

❀ After sewing the looped fringe around the flap and assembling the purse as directed in the pattern, proceed with the following flap trim.

1. Sew, hand-stitch, or glue with fabric glue the feather trim around the flap. Follow this with the eyelash trim over the feather trim.

2. Stitch and glue turquoise stones in place, using the small beads or roundels as stopper beads to attach the turquoise stones.

3. Using industrial-strength glue, adhere beaded stars in place. Using fabric glue, adhere the flat braid trim over top edges of looped and feather trims.

❀ Make rolled strap, following the instructions for the pattern. Set aside until ready to place and stitch.

High Tea

I'll have some cream and butter, si vous plait; and please, some of those exotic pink flowers for my table. I do so love soft things and pale colors. This lovely purse of finest silk is an adornment on its own with the added sparkle of a removable flower brooch.

Materials
- Cotton piping, ½" dia. (2 yds) for rolled strap
- Fusible fleece (½ yd)
- Fusible interfacing (¼ yd) for flap
- Lining fabric (½ yd)
- Pale gold embroidered silk with pink sheen (⅔ yd)
- Pale gold looped fringe, ½"-wide (3 yds)

Embellishment
- Removable brooch

Pattern and Instructions

Refer to Pattern 1 on pages 99–101. If you prefer to use different fabrics and trims than those listed above, use the generic list of materials listed with the pattern.

Corner detail

Design Tips

❀ Make the rolled strap, following instructions for the pattern. Set aside until ready to place and stitch.

❀ If your fabric is not as embroidered as the fabric used on this purse, you can easily add additional embellishments, such as flat braid over the seams covering the header of the looped fringe.

❀ If you are using a fabric that is heavier than silk, you may prefer to attach multiple brooches on the flap.

Inside pocket detail

Mon Cheri!

Who could resist this bag of soft, melting colors? The scent of rose petals and honeysuckle linger. So very French, mon cheri! Feathery edges and rose pink cord form a beautiful setting for the one-of-a-kind handmade porcelain brooch. This carefully thought-out bag brings the past near.

Materials
- Contrasting silk (⅓ yd)
- Cord (1½ yds) plus (½ yd) for drawstrings
- Fusible fleece (⅓ yd)
- Hand-beaded strap (26")
- Industrial-strength glue
- Silk lining fabric (⅓ yd)
- Small buttons to secure strap (2)
- Vintage pink silk brocade, 9" x 27"

Embellishments
- Beaded porcelain brooch
- Fabric-covered button, 1¼"
- Silver metal cord ends (2)

Pattern and Instructions

Refer to Pattern 8 on pages 116–117. You will find the instructions are complete and give instruction/ materials for both large and medium size purses—this design is the medium size.

If you prefer to use different fabrics and trims than those listed above, use the generic list of materials listed with the pattern.

Bottom view

Design Tips

✿ This fabulous vintage silk brocade is the perfect background for special accents such as the beaded porcelain brooch and the beaded strap.

✿ The contrasting silk chosen for the top and bottom of the purse is designed with rows of different textures and colors of silk. The torn edges of the green silk prove to be especially intriguing. Searching for special fabrics to use in your purses is worth the time and effort.

Vanity Fair

Oh, you sweet thing! Take my hand and say you'll be mine forever. I love your silky plaid dress with its swishy trim and the crystals that sparkle like your eyes. I'll be taking you to the poshest parties and all the best restaurants and shops.

Materials
- Embroidered silk fabric (⅜ yd)
- Industrial-strength glue
- Lining (¼ yd)
- Looped fringes: main color, ½"-wide (1⅓ yds); contrasting color, ½"-wide (⅔ yd)
- Zipper, 7"

Embellishments
- Rhinestones (12)

Pattern and Instructions
Refer to Pattern 6 on pages 112–113. If you prefer to use different fabrics and trims than those listed above, use the generic list of materials listed with the pattern.

Strap detail

A Little Romance

Chapter 4

These purses are small—like a fine jewel that does not have to overwhelm to impress. They are delicate sonatas as played softly on a piano, not the full sound of an orchestra. A small sigh with a loud message, these little bags are perfect for stepping out on the town dressed to the nines. Yet they are sophisticated enough so that one need not speak to command attention.

Meticulous detailing on fine fabrics is the high note for any little romance. The rich royal colors add to the beauty and mystery that only romance can bring.

Polka Dance

Don't you just love polka dots? They have such energy. All this and the froufrou on the front make this bag seem to dance all by itself.

Materials
- Black flat scalloped trim, ¼"-wide (1½ yds)
- Black moiré fabric (½ yd)
- Chocolate/black polka dots taffeta (⅔ yd)
- Fusible fleece (½ yd)
- Fusible interfacing (¼ yd)

Embellishments
- Beaded fringe, 1¼"-wide (½ yd)
- Black eyelash trim, 3"-wide (½ yd)
- Black velvet flower, 3" dia.
- Organdy and feather flowers, 3" dia. (2)
- Pin backs (3) (optional)

Pattern and Instructions
Finished size is 8½" x 11". Refer to Pattern 1 on pages 99–101. If you prefer to use different fabrics and trims than those listed above, use the generic list of materials listed with the pattern.

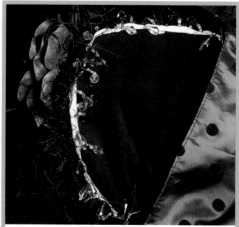

Inside flap detail

Design Tips

❀ Sew black braid in the seam for a nice scalloped finish around the body and the flap.

❀ Hand-stitch beaded fringe and black eyelash trim around flap.

❀ Stitch, pin, or glue the velvet flower in the center of the flap and organdy/ feather pieces on either side of the flower.

❀ The 24" strap is the same taffeta; line this with black moiré fabric.

Fringe Benefits

"Don't be cruel." Of course, we would never do that. This little bag is "crewel" of a different sort. Black wool is worked with rich deep colors. To enhance the floral theme, a handmade rose draws the eye to the ombre of long fringe.

Materials
- Black wool floral crewel (½ yd)
- Fusible fleece (⅓ yd)
- Hand-dyed silky fringe, 7"-wide (½ yd)
- Lavender/black silk lining fabric (½ yd)
- Matching chain with catches (1⅓ yds) for attaching to purse
- Matching eyelash fringe, 3"-wide (1⅓ yds)
- Purse frame with rods, antique silver finish, 7"-wide

Embellishments
- Heat fusible crystals (40–50)

Cabbage Rose
- Bar pin back
- Black felt circles, 2½" dia. (2)
- Burgundy/green eyelash fringe, 3"-wide (½ yd)
- Burgundy looped fringe, 3"-wide (½ yd)
- Glues: fabric; industrial-strength

Pattern and Instructions
Refer to Pattern 14 on pages 130–131. Sew 7" fringe to bottom of right side of purse front before making purse. After purse is constructed, use fabric glue or stitch eyelash trim along bottom of the purse and over the header of the 7" fringe. If you prefer to use different fabrics and trims than those listed above, use the generic list of materials listed with the pattern.

Cabbage Rose detail

Design Tips
❁ Follow the instructions for the pattern to make the blossom. Hand- or machine-stitch eyelash trim to edge of folded and sewn looped fringe.

❁ Heat-fuse the crystals scattered about the hand-bag and every 1½" on exposed eyelash on the Cabbage Rose.

Brown-eyed Princess

Surely this silk once pillowed the head of a brown-eyed princess. This delicate fragment, with embroidered and three-dimensional flowers and leaves, is truly textile art. This glorious little purse, like most things of quality, is as beautiful on the back as on the front.

Materials
- Contrasting antique embroidered silk (scrap)
- Fusible fleece (⅓ yd)
- Glues: fabric; industrial-strength
- Gold/bronze silk fabric (⅓ yd)
- Gold/bronze silk lining fabric (⅓ yd)
- Purse frame with handle, 6"-wide

Embellishments
- Antique millinery silk flower
- Coral beads for purse frame
- Coral beads for silk flower trim
- Silk flower trim, ¼"-wide (1½ yds)

Pattern and Instructions
Refer to Pattern 16 on page 133. If you prefer to use different fabrics and trims than those listed above, use the generic list of materials listed with the pattern.

Back view

Design Tips

❀ Add the coral beads to the purse frame and again on the floral border for that extra-special touch. Use industrial-strength glue to attach the beads. Take care that the glue does not show.

❀ Carry the same design around to the back side of this purse, with the exception of the antique blossom in the corner of the blue on the front side.

❀ If the vintage blue silk piece is fragile, fuse fleece to the back of the piece, then appliqué it to the purse. *Note: If you prefer to have the entire bag fused with fleece and need a stabilizer for your vintage silk piece, you may use a very lightweight interfacing and use the fleece on the inside of the purse body.*

❀ Glue vintage millinery roses that match the silk embroidery over the fragile places.

Gypsy

This is definitely not your basic black. This black is enhanced by someone who loves vivid color and motion. The net background is jumping with hot colors and the fringe is topped with black crystals.

Materials
- Black looped fringe, ½"-wide (1½ yds)
- Black netting/silk ribbon fabric (⅓ yd)
- Black silk lining fabric (⅓ yd)
- Black velvet scalloped trim, ½"-wide (1½ yds)
- Fabric glue
- Fusible fleece (¼ yd)
- Gold metallic ribbon, ½"-wide (½ yd)
- Gold-tone chain (44")
- Gold-tone purse frame with rods, 4¾"-wide
- Metallic gold trim, ¼"-wide (1 yd)

Embellishments
- Black faceted beads (30)
- Black velvet/gold metallic blossom

Pattern and Instructions

Refer to Pattern 9 on page 118. You will find the instructions are complete—there are no pattern pieces for this purse. Construction requires only specific size rectangles of fabric which are described in the pattern instructions. If you prefer to use different fabrics and trims than those listed above, use the generic list of materials listed with the pattern.

Back view

Design Tips

❀ The fabric chosen for this small purse is delightful. The body of the purse is made from black silk netting that is embroidered with bright, cheerful colors of silk ribbon. *Note: This is not vintage fabric and should be available in your fabric shops.* The black/gold blossom embellishment is made with black velvet trim and gold metallic trim. To make the mums, follow instructions in Pattern 15 on page 132.

❀ Black faceted beads are sewn 1" apart around the gold metallic ribbon at the top of the black looped fringe.

The Casbah

Edges rippling with ribbon and crystal beads, this black silk fabric is embroidered in an overall pattern of shapes and swirls. The colors are gently whispering "come hither." Drawn by the genteel fabric, one notices endearing details. The frame is embellished with swirls that mirror the fabric and is trimmed with dainty net roses.

Materials
- Black embroidered silk (¼ yd)
- Black flat scalloped trim, ½"-wide (⅔ yd)
- Black moiré lining fabric (¼ yd)
- Fabric glue
- Gold chain (1⅔ yds)
- Gold purse frame with holes, 4½"-wide
- Metallic trim, ¼"-wide (⅓ yd)
- Organza and embroidered flower trim, ¾"-wide (⅓ yd)

Pattern and Instructions
Refer to Pattern 17 on page 134. If you prefer to use different fabrics and trims than those listed above, use the generic list of materials listed with the pattern.

Flower trim detail

Design Tips

❋ When attaching purse to frame, remember the inside and outside will be seen. Use metallic trim to cover the frame on the inside of the purse and the flower trim on the outside of the frame to give the purse a finished look.

❋ Sew the black flat scalloped trim into the seam around the body, stopping at the marks on the pattern for the start of the frame.

Gwinevere's Cloak

The touch of burnout velvet, that convergence of sheer and plush, awakens a mystery in me and romantic fantasies fill my head. Surely this marvelous material came from Gwinevere's cloak that she wore to please her Arthur.

Materials
- Burgundy burnout velvet (½ yd)
- Burgundy looped fringe, ½"-wide (½ yd)
- Burgundy silk or satin lining fabric (½ yd)
- Fabric glue
- Matching chain (48")
- Purse frame with rods, 7½"-wide
- Sequin and ribbon trim (½ yd)

Embellishment
- Large burgundy velvet blossom

Pattern and Instructions
Finished size is 9" x 12". Refer to Pattern 14 on pages 130–131. If you prefer to use different fabrics and trims than those listed above, use the generic list of materials listed with the pattern.

Velvet blossom detail

Design Tips

❋ The burnout velvet is over-dyed for an interesting finish. We used a custom-order velvet blossom, looped fringe, and sequin trim that matched the darker burgundy in the fabric. This gave the purse a rich and elegant finish.

❋ All trims and embellishments are added to the finished body construction.

Tosca

You have good seats for Puccini's beautiful "Tosca." What is Italy without the arts? The voices of the crowd entering the hall mix with the orchestra tuning their instruments and you feel that unique thrill. Clutching your black tapestry bag, you feel as gorgeous as the beautiful Tosca herself.

Materials
- Black/design Italian tapestry (½ yd)
- Black silk lining fabric (½ yd)
- Brass chain (39")
- Brass purse frame with rods, 7½"-wide
- Fusible fleece (⅓ yd)
- Harvest gold flat rayon trim, ¾"-wide (¾ yd)
- Harvest gold looped fringe, 3"-wide (1⅔ yds)

Pattern and Instructions

Refer to Pattern 14 on pages 130–131. If you prefer to use different fabrics and trims than those listed above, use the generic list of materials listed with the pattern.

Fringe angle detail

Design Tips

❀ The looped fringe is stitched diagonally around front and back, starting with the bottom row and finishing with the flat rayon trim over the looped fringe header.

❀ This purse frame is easy to use, as the rods just slip through fabric channels (much like curtains on a curtain rod). Some frames require more advanced sewing skills.

❀ When working with a tapestry fabric, take care to not compete with the design by overembellishing it.

Apple Blossom

This purse reminds one of spring and apple blossoms. The chartreuse silk is embroidered with pink vines and abloom with multihued dots. The prissy ruffles are made sassier by the addition of tiny pink ruffled edging. A purse to be twirled and flaunted, this charming confection even wears a spray of pink beads.

Materials
- Chain (39")
  (optional)
- Fancy embroidered
  silk (1 yd)
- Fusible fleece (¼ yd)
- Purse frame with bar,
  7½"-wide
- Ruffled trim, ½"-wide
  (4 yds)
- Silk lining fabric
  (⅜ yd)

Embellishments
- Inexpensive acrylic
  bead chokers (2)
- Small (not tiny)
  beads (100)
- Your choice of
  embellishments

Pattern and Instructions
Refer to Pattern 7 on pages 114–115.

Delicate Enchantment

Chapter 5

Lace wedding dresses, christening gowns, and luxurious lingerie are associated with special times. Only lace will do for such occasions. Why is lace so special? Its enchantment comes from the patterns formed by what is not there. It has holes! They have not been cut out, but rather the lace is woven in patterns of openwork. The finer designs are the most expensive, but not always the most sought after. Each cherished design has its own unique beauty. A lace purse adds delicate enchantment to a wardrobe.

Tussy Mussy

Tomorrow and tomorrow and tomorrow—you will enjoy this dainty bag that comes from yesterdays. The dip and sway of the waltz will show off the antique wedding tussy mussy and ripple the fine lace across the bottom. The strap is the perfect finish, made of carved beads.

Materials
- Antique lace or lace collar, 2"-wide (⅔ yd)
- Carved stone beads, ½" dia. (35) for strap
- Carved stone rose beads, ⅝" dia. (6) for strap
- Fusible fleece (¼ yd)
- Gold chain (39") (optional)
- Iridescent embroidered silk (⅓ yd)
- Lace with wooden beads, 1"-wide not including beads (1½ yds)
- Purse frame with rods, 5½"-wide
- Silk or moiré taffeta (⅓ yd)
- Small wooden beads (14) for trim on strap
- Strap attachments (2)
- Wooden beads, ⅝" dia. (8) for trim on strap

Embellishments
- Antique millinery corsage
- Fabric glue
- Heavy lace, 7"–8" sq.
- Pin back
- Ribbon, ⅜"-wide (1 yd)
- Vintage Tussy Mussy
- Wool felt, 3" x 6"

Pattern and Instructions

Refer to Pattern 18 on pages 135–136. If you prefer to use different fabrics and trims than those listed above, use the generic list of materials listed with the pattern. This specific design has the following additional steps not found with the pattern.

Design Tips

❀ The beaded lace trim and corsage lace are dipped in strong coffee to create an antiqued look.

❀ For the Tussy Mussy—cut two 3" felt circles. Gather up lace square in center. Sew heavy lace to one felt circle, stitching it down in places and pleating where necessary to form a nice background for the antique millinery corsage.

❀ After lace and corsage are stitched and glued in place, finish with the pin back on the remaining felt circle, covering the first circle.

❀ To make the 24" beaded strap, alternate four wooden beads and three carved stone roses, followed with 35 carved stone ½" beads. Finish strap with wooden beads and carved roses to match opposite side. Sew ends firmly to strap attachments and secure with fabric glue.

1. Hand-stitch collar and beaded trim around purse sides and bottom.

2. Hand-stitch beaded trim across top of front, just below bottom casing seam.

Beaded Beauty

Your imagination is on fire and in your sewing box are two black lace collars beaded with colorful flowers. They are neither quaint nor dainty, but evocative of some black and daring gown. This is definitely Scarlet not Millie! It will make a spectacular statement of your personal taste, fine but not tame.

Materials
- Antique beaded lace collars (2)
- Black velvet (⅔ yd) for body
- Glues: fabric; industrial-strength
- Hand-strung seed beads (¼ yd)
- Looped rayon fringes, ½"-wide (2 yds each): black, red
- Magnet snap
- Red silk lining fabric (⅔ yd)

Embellishment
- Black drop-bead fringe, ½"-wide (⅓ yd)

Pattern and Instructions

Refer to Pattern 1 on pages 99–101. The pattern was altered to create a squared flap, but the construction is as described in the pattern. If you prefer to use different fabrics and trims than those listed above, use the generic list of materials listed with the pattern.

Design Tips

❀ Change the shape of the flap on the pattern to accommodate the antique beaded collar. The basic flap shape in the pattern will be just as effective.

❀ Use the collar in the best condition on the flap. The remaining collar can then be cut out and used as an accent in the lower corner of the bag front.

❀ This purse has three rows of looped fringe around the body, two black and one red sandwiched in between. The flap has one row of red under one row of black sewn along the bottom edge of the flap. The flap is topped off with black beaded trim.

Inside flap detail

Hearts & Flowers

Remember trying to make valentines with paper lace, colored paper, and glitter? I never understood why I was disappointed every time; but now I do. I wanted it to look like this—a mixture of magic and alchemy. The vintage fabric and lace have been dyed and overdyed to achieve a rich depth of color. Mixed with trailing ribbons, eyelash fringe, and sparkling hearts, it has become the valentine of my dreams.

Materials
- Antique silver chain (42")
- Fusible fleece (½ yd)
- Fusible interfacing (¼ yd)
- Glues: fabric; industrial-strength
- Hand-dyed crocheted lace, 1"-wide (1 yd)
- Hand-dyed crocheted sailor collar, 8" x 10"
- Hand-dyed crocheted snowflake, 5" dia.
- Magnetic strip
- Overdyed damask (½ yd) for purse and lining
- Purple eyelash fringe (1 yd)

Embellishments
- Felt circle, 3" dia.
- Hand-dyed crocheted flowers, 3" dia. (3)
- Iridescent heart beads (18)
- Vintage grosgrain ribbons, ½"-wide (2 yds each): green, purple

Pattern and Instructions

Refer to Pattern 1 on pages 99–101. The pattern was altered to fit the crocheted collar, but the basic construction follows the pattern instructions. The 1" lace is sewn into the purse and flap seams.

If you prefer to use different fabrics and trims than those listed above, use the generic list of materials listed with the pattern.

Back view

Design Tips

❀ Sew and/or glue heart beads along flap and on purse.

❀ Cut the three crocheted flowers from one side to center to form corsage. Stitch eyelash around center of flowers. Coil flowers around felt circle to form a layered corsage. Adhere heart beads in center. Glue directly to the purse.

❀ Hand-stitch hand-dyed crocheted snowflake to back of purse, and chain to top of side seams.

❀ Cut ribbons in half, using two colors on each side. Sew to area of side seam and chain. Tie a bow and stitch the knot a few times to secure. Trim to desired length.

Buttoned Up!

This exquisite confection could become a signature accessory and a prize for future generations. The white wool body is substantial enough to support the tinkling trim of button after button. Everything about this purse speaks elegance, and nothing says it more than the fabulous button-encrusted heart pinned on the turned-down cuff.

Materials
- Button fringe, 1¼"-wide (¾ yd)
- Cream heavy wool (⅔ yd)
- Cream moiré lining fabric (⅓ yd)
- Fabric glue
- Fusible fleece (⅓ yd)
- Heavy open lace, 4"-wide (25")
- Magnetic snap
- Ostrich fringe, 2½"-wide (¾ yd)

Embellishments
- Antique button brooch
- Assorted mother-of-pearl buttons for body and strap

Pattern and Instructions

Refer to Pattern 11 on pages 121–122. The ostrich fringe is stitched into cuff and purse seams. The button fringe is hand-stitched along the seam line. The heavy lace is hand-stitched and glued with fabric glue.

If you prefer to use different fabrics and trims than those listed above, use the generic list of materials listed with the pattern.

Button heart detail

Design Tips

❀ The turned-down cuff on this design is covered with wonderful heavy open lace. This white-on-white bag would make the perfect accessory for a winter wedding.

❀ Use a wide variety of buttons and baubles to give added interest and dimension to the purse.

Wedding Party

Surely this is the stuff dreams are made of. Lace of this type is costly and difficult to make, but a little goes a long way. The vintage still life of the Floppy Flower with celestial beads and crystals nestled near the top allows the bottom of the purse to swing out like a fine petticoat under a ball gown.

Materials
- Antique laces: 3"-wide (1⅓ yds); 6"-wide (3 yds)
- Chain to match (39") (optional)
- Fusible fleece (¼ yd)
- Purse frame with bar, 7½"-wide
- Silk or moiré taffeta lining fabric (1 yd)

Embellishments
- Felt circles, 2" dia. (2)

Floppy Flower
- Glues: fabric; industrial-strength
- Gold looped fringe, ½"-wide (½ yd)
- Lace, 2"-wide (½ yd)
- Vintage pearl/crystal cluster

Pattern and Instructions
Refer to Pattern 14 on pages 130–131. If you prefer to use different fabrics and trims than those listed above, use the generic list of materials listed with the pattern.

Use the basic pattern with the following additional steps for the layers of lace.

Continued on page 68

Design Tips

❀ To make the Floppy Flower, follow the instructions in Pattern 15 on page 135 with the following changes:

1. Use looped fringe and lace as close to the color of your purse lace as possible. Sew 2"-wide lace to header of looped fringe.

2. Coil and stitch to one of the felt circles. Clip lace in several places and tack it down as needed.

3. Glue and stitch vintage bead cluster to flower center.

❀ Make the chain detachable, as there may be special occasions when a hand-carried purse is more appropriate.

Wedding Party *continued*

1. Cut two front and two back pieces from the lining fabric to be used as the body fabric and the lining.

2. After you have followed the pattern through fusing fleece to front and back of the lining, stitch along the sides, about 7" on each side. Leave bottom and top open, making it easier to stitch the lace pieces on the body of the bag. Press seams and turn right side out. Repeat with the same fabric for the purse body.

3. Cut the 6" lace into two pieces, one a few inches longer than the other.

4. Sew the ends of the longer piece of lace together. Press and turn. Repeat with shorter piece of lace.

5. Sew a gathering stitch along the topside of each piece and gather.

6. Place smaller piece along lower part of purse. *Note: The bottom of the lace should be even with the raw seam of the lining.*

7. Pin lace top straight across purse front and back, then stitch in place.

8. Pin longer piece of lace along the top, about 1" below the casing stitching line. Overlap the bottom layer of lace about 4", then stitch in place.

9. Sew a piece of 3"-wide lace over outside of casing as described in the pattern and make a flounce at the top as seen in the photograph on page 67 with the scalloped edge on the lace extending above the casing fold.

10. Cut two pieces from 3"-wide lace, 13" long. Roll hems of each end.

11. Stitch these just beneath the first stitch line of the casing.

12. Place lining inside purse body and form casing, following instructions in the pattern.

13. Center and attach Floppy Flower to top front.

Floppy Flower detail

Some Things Never Change

Chapter 6

Like a woman who ages gracefully, a beautiful fabric will continue to be beautiful. Styles change, fashions come and go, but the best ones remain fresh and desirable.

These bags, made of well-preserved fabrics, are vintage in design and provide a striking background for lovely antique adornments. They dress up or down to suit your occasion or reflect your mood. They can be prim and proper or fresh and flirtatious. So don't be surprised when your daughter borrows one because even she knows that some things never change.

Madame Marie

A sumptuous piece of vintage drapery in the softest blend of colors, silky fringe, and romantic styling transports us directly to Marie Antoinette's France. We haven't forgotten her love of the finer things. Here, we find beautiful black tassels, trims, buttons, and beading, all mixed with velvet and pulled together with vintage metallic cord.

Materials
- Bead pearl drop fringe, 1"-wide (1 yd)
- Black flat trim, ½"-wide (2 yds)
- Black moiré lining fabric, 45"-wide (13")
- Black velvet (½ yd)
- Black vintage fringe, 3½"-wide at widest point (2 yds)
- Cord, ⅛" dia. (20")
- Fusible fleece, 13" x 45"
- Glues: fabric; industrial-strength
- Vintage black fabric, 13" x 32"
- Vintage metallic cord, ¼" dia. (3½ yds)

Embellishments
- Antique black buttons, ½" (2); 1"
- Rectangular oriental black beads (2)
- Tiny black beads (2)
- Victorian beaded tassel (2)

Pattern and Instructions
Refer to Pattern 8 on pages 116–117. If you prefer to use different fabrics and trims than those listed above, use the generic list of materials listed with the pattern.

Vintage cord detail

Design Tips

❀ Select a fabric with black accents to make this purse more dramatic.

❀ If you can't find vintage metallic cord, use black cord for the drawstring.

❀ Black silk tassels can be used in place of the Victorian beaded tassels.

Bonbon

This bag is a delicious bonbon to seemingly melt in your mouth and perhaps melt your heart. A lovely confection of mellowed French fabric, all buttery and soft, painted in pinks and rose, and embellished with delicious colors of yesteryear's fringe. The delightful final ingredient is a celluloid button polished by time to perfection.

Materials
- Cotton cord, (1⅓ yds) for strap
- Fusible fleece (¼ yd)
- Silk lining fabric (¾ yd) for strap
- Vintage French drapery (¼ yd)
- Vintage pink fringe with rose header, 1½"-wide (1 yd)
- Vintage soft yellow fringe, 1½"-wide (1 yd)

Fringe detail

Embellishment
- Large vintage celluloid button

Pattern and Instructions
Refer to Pattern 1 on pages 99–101. If you prefer to use different fabrics and trims than those listed above, use the generic list of materials listed with the pattern.

Design Tips

❋ We were thrilled when we found these wonderful vintage draperies from France in an interesting butter yellow with touches of pink, rose, and olive. We had enough fabric in excellent condition to make several purses from one panel. Estate sales are a great place to find this kind of fabric.

❋ Make it a habit to visit small-town antique shops that carry vintage trims and brooches. You will be thrilled when you find something wonderful like the vintage fringe seen on this lovely purse.

❋ We created a rolled strap from the lining material for this purse by following the pattern instructions. A flat strap could also be made from the vintage fabric. *Note: If you decide to make the flat strap, you will not need the cotton cord. If you want the flat strap from the body fabric, as opposed to the lining fabric, add ½ yard to the body fabric and delete same amount from the lining fabric.*

❋ Stitch the vintage yellow fringe inside the seams on the body and the flap. Hand-stitch pink fringe with a rose header around body, then machine-stitch it on the flap.

Sweet Magnolia

"A rose by any other name is still a rose." Certainly this is true of our full-blown beauty surrounded by velvet leaves and petals of burgundy. Which came first, the rose corsage or the perfect background fabric of a "certain age?" The ruffly burgundy trim is a perfect enclosure for our enchanted garden, which grows green glass hearts among the flowers.

Materials
- Burgundy silk pleated ruffling, 1"–2"-wide (3 yds)
- Cotton cord, ½" dia. (1½ yd) for strap
- Fusible fleece (⅓ yd)
- Fusible interfacing (¼ yd)
- Magnetic snap
- Sage green rayon flat trim, ½"-wide (1½ yds)
- Silk (¾ yd) for lining and bias rolled strap
- Vintage French chenille drapery (⅓ yd)

Embellishments
- Tiny gold beads (20)
- Vintage corsage
- Vintage green glass hearts (20)

Pattern and Instructions
Refer to Pattern 2 on pages 102–104. If you prefer to use different fabrics and trims than those listed above, use the generic list of materials listed with the pattern.

Inside flap detail

Design Tips

❋ Pin corsage on flap after bag is completed to make it removable for multiple uses.

❋ Choose trims in the same color tones that are repeated in the large corsage.

❋ Sew the burgundy pleated ruffling in the seams around the body and flap.

❋ Hand-stitch the sage trim around the purse body. When stitching the same trim around the flap, an antique glass heart is sewn every inch. To attach the hearts, use needle and thread through the glass heart, through a tiny gold bead, back through the heart, and secure to the sage trim.

Vintage Nosegay

A trifle is my very favorite dessert—layers of one delicious thing after another, left to meld a couple of days. This very romantic purse is like that. The base is a pale barkcloth, then a flurry of yesterday's laces, vintage satin leaves, and—the frosting on the cake—marvelous chenille embroidered roses in wonderfully edible colors. As you can see, this is no mere trifle, it's dessert.

Materials
- Fabric glue
- Matching chain (39")
- Silk lining fabric (½ yd)
- Silver tone purse frame with rods, 7½"-wide
- Vintage muted print drapery fabric (½ yd)

Embellishments
- Sequin trim, ½"-wide (½ yd)
- Vintage embroidered chenille blossoms (3)
- Vintage off-white cotton lace, 1"-wide (½ yd)
- Vintage satin handmade petals (5)
- Vintage tiny metallic cord (1 yd)

Pattern and Instructions
Refer to Pattern 14 on pages 130–131. If you prefer to use different fabrics and trims than those listed above, use the generic list of materials listed with the pattern.

Design Tips

❋ To make the pictured nosegay embellishment, construct five petals from a coordinating color in soft satin or a metallic fabric.

1. Cut five ovals 3" long and 1½" wide. Fold the oval in half lengthwise and run a gathering stitch along the open curved edge. Pull the gathering thread tight to form the petal.

2. Arrange petals in center of front and hand-stitch or glue in place.

3. Make small loops from metallic cord by making two three-ply cord bows secured in the center with thread. Place these bows randomly to add dimension. Stitch or glue flowers in center of petal base.

4. Frame entire nosegay with vintage cotton lace stitched in an oval shape. Cover edge of lace with sequin embroidered trim.

❋ If you are unable to obtain vintage trims, a nosegay can be made from carefully chosen new materials. Just take care to select muted colors that blend with your chosen fabric.

Lady of Spain

A dash of mystery and intrigue—the portrait of a beautiful woman. Is this someone I know or did I meet her in a dream? I see upon closer inspection the dress of antique paisley and a hat of velvet and ostrich trimmed with stunning black beaded ornaments. Do you know who she is?

Materials

- Antique buttons (2) for attaching strap
- Antique wool piano shawl (⅔ yd)
- Black looped fringe, ½"-wide (1½ yds)
- Black ostrich trim
- Crushed red velvet (scrap)
- Dark red silk lining fabric (1 yd)
- Dark red velvet, 6" x 12" for flap lining
- Fusible fleece (⅔ yd)
- Fusible interfacing 3" sq. (2)
- Industrial-strength glue
- Magnetic snap
- Narrow beaded black velvet braid (18")
- Narrow black silk ribbon
- Red looped fringe, ½"-wide (3 yds)

Embellishments

- Antique black beaded balls
- Black felt oval to back brooch
- Lady portrait brooch
- Polymer clay face

Pattern and Instructions

Refer to Pattern 2 on page 102–104. If you prefer to use different fabrics and trims than those listed above, use the generic list of materials listed with the pattern.

Design Tips

✿ Following the manufacturer's directions for polymer clay, shape a face by forming it on the back of a teaspoon, then baking as directed. *Note: The flat-back porcelain faces are available in embellishment shops. These will work just as the polymer clay faces.*

1. Using a micron pen, draw facial features. Add color to cheeks and eyes with crayons.

2. Using industrial-strength glue, attach face to black felt oval, leaving a rim of felt around face to use in adding embellishments.

3. To make it a detachable brooch, add a bar pin to back of felt oval to attach brooch to purse. Or, attach face and embellishments directly to flap of bag before lining flap.

4. Frame the face with a crushed velvet "hat," then trim with a few pieces of eyelash fringe and other embellishments below the velvet.

5. Finish with a small ribbon and drop beads under the chin and for earrings.

✿ Use fabric glue or hand-stitching to attach narrow black beaded trim around flap.

Cut Flowers

Just as you have never forgotten the sounds and the mists of the rain forest, this extravagant blossom growing abundantly among giant ferns and unnamed flora has stayed in your mind. What a delight to find it worked in silk thread by another smitten traveler. No need to look further for exotic mementos. Here are large yellow jade treasures and beads of rose and cream mixed with fine old fringe and fabric.

Materials
- Butter yellow vintage silk fringe, 1½"-wide (1½ yds)
- Embroidered appliqué for flap
- Flat apricot trim, ¼"-wide (1½ yds)
- Fusible interfacing, 3"-wide (2)
- Fusible medium-weight fleece (⅓ yd)
- Lining fabric (⅓ yd)
- Magnetic snap
- Metallic fabric or silk (¼ yd) for flap
- Short apricot vintage silk fringe, ¾"-wide (1½ yds)
- Silk flower trim, ½"-wide (¾ yd)
- Vintage French drapery fabric (⅓ yd)

Embellishments
- Flat brass roundels (6)
- Large yellow jade beads (2)
- Small rose horn beads (14)

Bead Strap:
- Beading needle
- Brass necklace fasteners (2)
- Brass rings, ⅜" dia. (2)
- Cream beads (36)
- Fabric glue
- Flat brass roundels (4)
- Large yellow jade beads (2)
- Small rose horn flat beads (105)
- Strong waxed beading thread

Continued on page 82

Design Tips

✿ Vintage needlework, silk fringe, and draperies can be found in antique shops, flea markets, and garage sales. It may take some time to find all of the pieces in the colors you have chosen for your purse. All embellishments can be replaced with carefully chosen new items.

✿ The flap on this purse is constructed with a metallic fabric and overlaid with an antique embroidered appliqué. We used fusible fleece on the lining of this flap, as opposed to interfacing. *Note: This gives it more stability for the appliqué.*

Cut Flowers *continued*

Pattern and Instructions

Refer to Pattern 1 on pages 99–101. *Note: The yardage used on this purse design is slightly different than the standard yardage in the pattern. The use of the metallic fabric for the flap is the difference.*

1. The yellow fringe is stitched into the seam of the purse body and flap.

2. The apricot fringe is hand-stitched or glued along the edge of the seams or purse body and flap.

3. After the embroidered piece is glued and hand-stitched to the flap, the silk flower trim is hand-stitched along the edge of the apricot fringe on the flap.

If you prefer to use different fabrics and trims than those listed on page 80, use the generic list of materials listed with the pattern.

Beads detail

Design Tips

❀ The bead strap is detachable.

1. Use a strong waxed thread small enough to go through the bead holes without a needle. Thread them in the following order: brass roundel, yellow jade bead, brass roundel, cream bead, three rose flat beads, cream bead, then repeat until you have approximately 23".

2. Add a brass roundel, yellow jade bead and one more brass roundel. Tie off securely.

3. Place a bit of glue on the knot to secure. Sew brass rings to top of purse body seams. Attach strap.

❀ For bead embellishment, use a beading thread and needle to secure the piece to the center edge of the flap.

1. Thread a brass roundel, three rose beads, brass roundel, yellow jade bead, three rose beads, and one more brass roundel.

2. Take needle around last roundel and back through all of the beads. Stitch securely. Repeat for second bead dangle.

Everything Old Is New Again

Chapter 7

Can you hear the big-band sound of Glenn Miller playing In the Mood? Or, perhaps the lovely String of Pearls he wrote for his wife?

These purses will remind you of an era when women wore tightly fitted suits with beautiful accessories on the shoulder, stating that being capable and romantic were not mutually exclusive ideas.

Enjoy the purses made of nostalgic fabrics, each adorned by one-of-a-kind collages of old millinery pieces, floppy vintage flowers, and bits of wonderfulness that someone could not bear to part with— and now, these old things are new again.

Earth Echoes

A tailored suit, with discreet trim and the hint of a fine blouse underneath, is softened by a large, but not frivolous, shoulder ornament. This shows that you have a softer side, yes, but don't be fooled by the flower. You are not a shrinking violet.

Strap detail

Materials
- Brown faux suede fabric (½ yd)
- Burgundy faux suede fabric (⅙ yd)
- Cord, ⅛" dia. (2 yds) for piping
- Fusible fleece (⅜ yd)
- Fusible interfacing (¼ yd)
- Magnetic snap
- Tiny brown checkered silk lining fabric (½ yd)

Embellishments
- Bakelite pieces (2)
- Brown button, ½" dia.
- Large millinery flower brooch
- Vintage button, 1¼" dia.

Pattern and Instructions
Finished size is 12" x 10" x 3". Refer to Pattern 10 on pages 119–120. If you prefer to use different fabrics and trims than those listed above, use the generic list of materials listed with the pattern.

Optional Welted Pocket Back view
(pattern not included)

Thoroughly Modern Millie

Better practice that Charleston—the day of the flapper never really ended. Here is Nola herself, hand-painted on porcelain and surrounded with a flurry of velvet and metallic leaves. Effervescent fringe edges the hand-screened fabric and swings with the beat.

Materials
- Fusible fleece (¼ yd)
- Gold chain (39")
- Gold purse frame with rod to attach purse, 5"-wide
- Gold silk lining fabric (⅓ yd)
- Industrial-strength glue
- Red and gold silk-screened fabric (⅓ yd)
- Red hem tape (½ yd)
- Vintage gold fringe, ½-wide (1 yd)

Embellishments
- Assorted millinery velvet leaves
- Metallic and chenille trims (scraps)
- "Nola" flapper bas relief
- Small green feather
- Vintage metallic gold leaves

Pattern and Instructions

Refer to Pattern 9 on page 118. If you prefer to use different fabrics and trims than those listed above, use the generic list of materials listed with the pattern.

"Nola" detail

Design Tips

❃ The flapper head is technically known as a bas-relief head. In the old days, these were manufactured for use on boudoir items such as handkerchief sachets, on pincushions, and purses.

❃ The fabric is a red silky file fabric and that is silk-screened with gold leaves.

❃ The leaf design in the fabric is carried through in the flapper collage.

Kismet

Kiwi and burgundy—sounds like an inventive menu drink. Instead of a silly paper umbrella, it comes with a rich assortment of leaves and fabric centered by a sparkling pin. The trim is ostrich. Are you sure you came to the right cafe? This sizzles so much more than you expected.

Materials
- Camel wool (½ yd)
- Flat kiwi green trim, ½"-wide (¾ yd)
- Fusible fleece (⅓ yd)
- Kiwi green wool (⅓ yd)
- Lining fabric (⅓ yd)
- Magnetic snap
- Wine fringe, 2½"-wide (¾ yd)

Embellishments
- Corsage
- Large vintage buttons (2)

Pattern and Instructions
Refer to Pattern 19 on pages 137–138. If you prefer to use different fabrics and trims than those listed above, use the generic list of materials listed with the pattern.

Vintage button detail

Design Tips

❀ Make this delicate corsage with vintage millinery leaves and fabric, then center it on the cuff with a vintage brooch.

❀ Try your own corsage creation or substitute a dramatic new corsage of dried flowers and leaves from your favorite florist.

Animal Magnetism

Hey! It's a jungle out there! You know because you've been and not only survived, but brought back a trophy. You even snagged an exotic flower for some razzle-dazzle. This says, "I can do it—I'm not afraid." Carry this velvety purse to announce you are the ruling cat.

Materials
- Brown chenille trim, ¼"-wide (2½ yds)
- Brown faux suede cloth, 3" x 30" for strap
- Brown/black polka dots silk lining fabric (½ yd)
- Fusible fleece (½ yd)
- Fusible interfacing, 3" sq. (2)
- Industrial-strength glue
- Leopard print velvet (½ yd)
- Magnetic snap

Embellishments
- Felted wool balls (10)
- Vintage corsage

Pattern and Instructions
Refer to Pattern 12 on pages 123–125. If you prefer to use different fabrics and trims than those listed above, use the generic list of materials listed with the pattern.

Vintage corsage detail

Design Tips

❀ Choose a corsage of millinery leaves, flowers, vintage ribbon and a vintage buckle to embellish the bag.

❀ Sew a brown chenille trim in the seam around the gusset of the purse front and back for a nice scalloped finish.

❀ Green felted wool balls coordinate with the vintage leaves in the corsage. Sew this trim and the brown chenille trim in the seam around the flap.

Tuscan Sun

This fantastic, happy purse brings back memories of warm days in Rome where we leaned over the curb to eat watermelon slices. We walked the old town sampling the many flavors of gelato in rainbow colors seen on every corner, while history slowly seeped into our thoughts. Rome—where so much began.

Materials
- Brick/gold flat trim, ½"-wide (1⅝ yds)
- Brick/sage rayon looped fringe, ½"-wide (4⅛ yds)
- Brick Italian tapestry (⅔ yd)
- Fusible fleece (½ yd)
- Fusible interfacing (¼ yd) for flap and snap reinforcement
- Glues: fabric; industrial-strength
- Gold silk lining fabric (½ yd)
- Large magnetic snap
- Suede cloth, 3" x 30" for strap lining

Embellishments
- Jade green donuts (3)

Pattern and Instructions
Refer to Pattern 12 on pages 123–125. If you prefer to use different fabrics and trims than those listed above, use the generic list of materials listed with the pattern.

Refer to Pattern 12 on pages 123–125.

Design Tips

✽ Using two Italian tapestries and purchasing large rolls of both will allow you to make different designs from the same fabric.

✽ Coordinating flat rayon trims gives the looped fringe a finished look. After the body and flap are constructed, glue or hand-stitch this trim around the purse front and flap.

✽ To make jade stone donuts:

1. Cut a 5" piece from flat trim for the center of the donut. Tie a loose knot in the center of the trim and push the end through the donut hole, leaving the knot on the topside.

2. Trim ends, leaving enough to glue to back of donut, but not so much that they would show at the edges.

3. Using industrial-strength glue, secure ends to back of donut. Glue donut with a knot to the flap and at strap seams, if desired.

✽ This design has a gusset. Sew two rows of the fringe around the front of the purse body and one row around the purse back. Use two rows around the flap.

Roman Holiday

You love to wear festive colors and a lot of detail but you like it toned down a bit. The black gives this purse a little edge of sophisticated polish. You may be giddy with delight in St. Michael's Square, but still, there is your more serious side.

Materials
- Black silk lining fabric, 45"-wide (1⅔ yds)
- Flat trim, ½"-wide (40") for top of strap
- Fusible fleece (½ yd)
- Fusible interfacing (¼ yd)
- Harvest gold looped fringe, ½"-wide (3½ yds)
- Industrial-strength glue
- Italian tapestry, 60"-wide (1⅛ yds)
- Large magnetic snap
- Red looped fringe, ½"-wide (2 yds)
- Suede cloth, 3⅓" x 40" for strap

Embellishment
- Large carved cinnabar bead

Pattern and Instructions
Refer to Pattern 13 on pages 126–129. If you prefer to use different fabrics and trims than those listed above, use the generic list of materials listed with the pattern.

Strap detail

Design Tips

✽ This Italian tapestry is striking with the black background trimmed in festive colors of harvest gold and red.

✽ Sew and glue large cinnabar bead on flap, or replace it with a large interesting button.

Romantic Rome

The cacophony created by vendor carts rolling over ancient cobblestone works better than any alarm clock. Market is being set up so throw open your windows and lean out to see. There are flowers and fruits of every color, pastry and coffee, and best of all, romantic purses.

Materials
- Black looped fringe, 3"-wide (2 yds)
- Black suede cloth, 3⅓" x 40" for strap
- Brick Italian tapestry, 60"-wide (1⅛ yds)
- Fusible fleece (½ yd)
- Fusible interfacing (¼ yd)
- Gold silk lining fabric, 45"-wide (1⅛ yds)
- Harvest gold flat braid, ¾"-wide (2 yds)
- Harvest gold looped fringe, 3"-wide (3¼ yds)

Embellishment
- Jade stone donut

Pattern and Instructions
Refer to Pattern 13 on pages 126–129. If you prefer to use different fabrics and trims than those listed above, use the generic list of materials listed with the pattern.

Strap detail

Design Tips
❋ To make jade stone donuts:

1. Cut a 5" piece from flat trim for the center of the donut. Tie a loose knot in the center of the trim and push the end through the donut hole, leaving the knot on the topside.

2. Trim ends, leaving enough to glue to back of donut, but not so much that they would show at the edges.

3. Using industrial-strength glue, secure ends to back of donut. Glue donut with a knot to the flap and at strap seams, if desired.

Pattern Section   Chapter 8

Making a most exquisite romantic purse is possible, regardless of your sewing and craft skills. In previous chapters, we have shown you ideas for romantic purses. In this chapter, we hope to inspire you to create your own heirloom purse.

Each pattern gives a generic materials list needed to make a basic purse. Use the pattern and instructions straight from this section or alter it to create your one-of-a-kind purse.

Each pattern in this section lists which purses in the book were made with that particular pattern.

Pattern 1

Finished size is 8½" x 11"—not counting trim. Pattern assumes ½" seam allowances included in the pattern and seams are pressed open.

Materials

Note: This list is appropriate for a generic version of the pattern. See Materials and Embellishments lists that accompany the titled purse to make the specific design shown.

- Basic fabric (⅔ yd) for purse
- Cotton piping, ½" dia. (2 yd) for rolled strap
- Flat braid trim, ¾"-wide (30") for flat fabric strap
- Fusible interfacing (¼ yd) for flap
- Fusible medium-weight fleece (½ yd)
- Lining fabric (½ yd)
- Rayon looped fringe, 1½"-wide (3 yds)
- Suede cloth, 3" x 30" for flat strap lining

Preparation

1. Cut two pieces each of Front/Back pattern on page 101 from basic fabric, fusible fleece, and lining fabric.

2. Cut one piece each of Flap pattern on page 101 from basic fabric, fusible interfacing, and lining fabric.

3. (Optional.) Cut two pieces of Inside Pocket pattern on page 101 from lining fabric.

4. **Flat strap:** Cut one 4" x 30" piece each from basic fabric and interfacing for 1½" x 39" strap.

   Flat strap with braid trim: Cut 30" piece from flat braid to trim fabric strap.

Rolled strap: Cut one 3" x 30" piece from basic fabric on bias and a piece of ½" diameter cotton piping that is twice the length of the finished strap length.

Flat strap backed with suede cloth: Cut one 3" x 30" piece from basic fabric to match suede cloth.

Construction

1. Following manufacturer's directions, fuse fleece to wrong side of basic fabric front, back, and flap. *Note: Use fleece in all silk and medium fabric purses. Use interfacing in flaps. Do not use interfacing in body of heavier weight fabrics.*

2. (Optional) Sew looped fringe or other trim to the right side of bag front. Place the header of the fringe along the outside edge of the bag front with the bottom of the fringe toward the center of the piece. If using multiple rows of fringe, sew the first color of fringe along the edge as described and second color on top of first row. *Note: Do not remove manufacturer's stabilizing thread along the bottom of the fringe until the fringe is stitched in place.*

3. With right sides together, sew front and back of bag together, leaving top open, and turn. *Note: Fringe or trim will now be around outside edge of sides and bottom.*

4. (Optional) Arrange flap embellishments that require stitching in place on right side of flap and stitch. *Note: If embellishments are to be glued in place, wait until flap is completed. Sew fringe or trim around flap, using same method as for purse body in Step 2.*

5. (Optional) Take the two pocket pieces cut from lining fabric, right sides together, sew across top, turn and press. Baste or pin around sides and bottom, sew to back lining just outside seam line. Assemble lining. Turn right side out and press.

6. (Optional) Place finished pocket on back lining, matching "X" on the pattern. Sew pocket to right side of back lining. Set aside.

7. Following manufacturer's instructions, attach the magnetic snap, matching the "X" on the purse front with the bag flap. Reinforce the area on purse front and flap lining with a 3" square of fusible interfacing. *Note: If using a regular snap, wait until purse construction is completed to add the snap.*

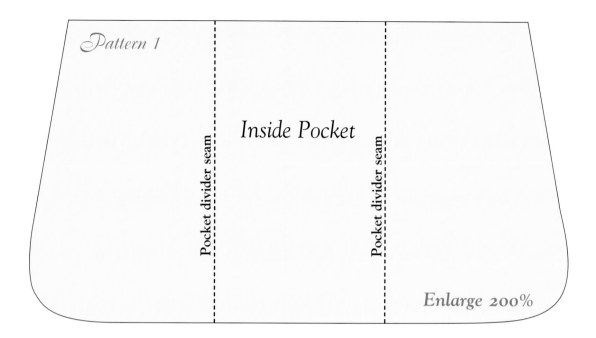

Pattern 1

Inside Pocket

Pocket divider seam

Pocket divider seam

Enlarge 200%

8. With right sides together, sew purse flap and flap lining together, leaving straight edge of flap open. Turn right side out and if you want a flat braid around the flap, sew it in place around the curved portion of the flap. *Note: If this is too thick for your machine, stitch in place by hand after purse is assembled.*

9. Make the strap as described below, then place the strap ends on the side seams inside the bag and sew in place.

Flat fabric strap: Fold fabric in half lengthwise. Sew along outside edge and press seam open. *Note: Sew across one end of strap, this makes turning easier and then you can snip this sewn end off after it is turned.* Turn and press flat with seam in center along bottom of strap.

Flat fabric strap with suede cloth underside: Turn under 1" on both sides of fabric and on both sides of suede cloth, then press. Place wrong sides together and edge-stitch with fabric on top and suede on bottom.

Rolled strap: Fold bias fabric, right sides together, and sew around cotton cord, leaving 29" of cord uncovered in front of fabric (left end of cord). Sew across cord at beginning of fabric to secure cord in place. Pull right end of cord, pushing fabric over left part of cord. *Note: The fabric will now be right side out when it is reversed and it will cover up the left side of the cord. Cut off exposed right side of cord.*

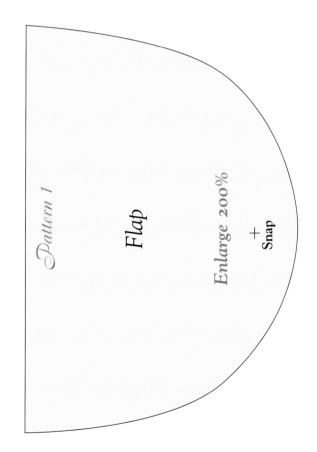

Pattern 1

Flap

Enlarge 200%

+ Snap

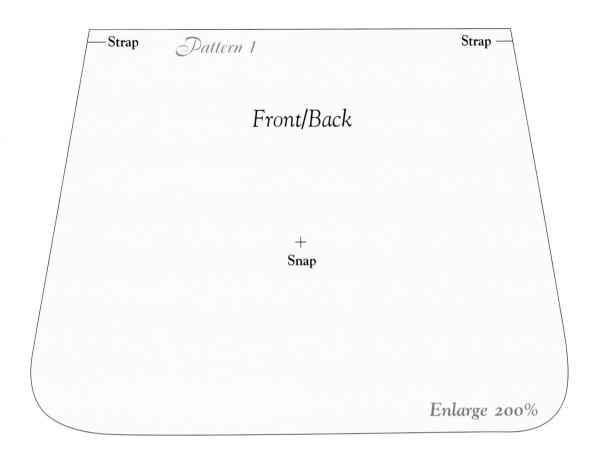

— Strap   *Pattern 1*   **Strap** —

Front/Back

+
Snap

Enlarge 200%

Pattern 1

Strap

Fold

Enlarge 200%

10. Turn in ½" seam allowance on bag and lining and either slip-stitch or topstitch along edge with sewing machine.

11. Center flap on back of bag and sew in place.

12. Slip bag inside lining with right sides together. Sew around top of bag, leaving open between

marks on top edge of pattern. Turn to right side, pushing lining into bag.

13. Adhere embellishments. See specific embellishment suggestions on the project page and the photograph of the bag you are making.

Pattern 2

Finished size is 9" x 13"—not counting trim. Pattern assumes ½" seam allowances included in the pattern and seams are pressed open.

Materials

Note: This list is appropriate for a generic version of the pattern. See Materials and Embellishments lists that accompany the titled purse to make the specific design shown.

- Basic fabric (¾ yd) for purse (⅔ yd if making a flat strap)
- Cotton piping, ½" dia.(2 yds) for rolled strap
- Flat braid trim, ¼"-wide (30") for flat strap with braid trim
- Fusible medium-weight fleece** (½ yd)
- Fusible interfacing (¼ yd) for flap
- Lining fabric(½ yd)
- Rayon looped fringe, ½"-long (4⅛ yds)
- Suede cloth, 3" x 30" for flat strap lining

** Fusible fleece is not necessary if your basic fabric is heavy-weight.

Preparation

1. Cut two pieces each of Front/Back pattern on page 104 from basic fabric, fusible fleece, and lining fabric.

2. Cut one piece each of Flap pattern below from basic fabric, fusible interfacing, and lining fabric.

3. (Optional.) Cut two pieces of Inside Pocket pattern on page 104 from lining fabric.

4. **Flat strap:** Cut one 4" x 30" piece each from basic fabric and interfacing for 1½" x 39" strap.

   Flat strap with braid trim: Cut 30" piece from flat braid to trim fabric strap.

   Rolled strap: Cut one 3" x 30" piece from basic fabric on bias and a piece of ½" diameter cotton piping that is twice the length of the finished strap length.

   Flat strap backed with suede cloth: Cut one 3" x 30" piece from basic fabric to match suede cloth.

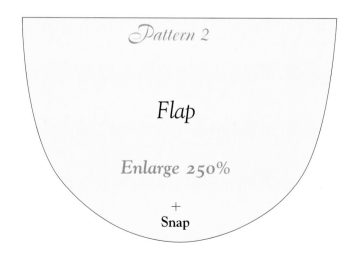

Pattern 2

Flap

Enlarge 250%

+
Snap

Construction

1. Following manufacturer's directions, fuse fleece to wrong side of basic fabric front, back, and flap. *Note: Use fleece in all silk and medium fabric purses. Use interfacing in flaps. Do not use interfacing in body of heavier weight fabrics.*

2. (Optional) Sew looped fringe or other trim to the right side of bag front. Place the header of the fringe along the outside edge of the bag front with the bottom of the fringe toward the center of the piece. If using multiple rows of fringe, sew the first color of fringe along the edge as described and second color on top of first row. *Note: Do not remove manufacturer's stabilizing thread along the bottom of the fringe until the fringe is stitched in place.*

3. With right sides together, sew front and back of bag together, leaving top open, and turn. *Note: Fringe or trim will now be around outside edge of sides and bottom.*

4. (Optional) Arrange flap embellishments that require stitching in place on right side of flap and stitch. *Note: If embellishments are to be glued in place, wait until flap is completed. Sew fringe or trim around flap, using same method as for purse body in Step 2.*

5. (Optional) Take the two pocket pieces cut from lining fabric, right sides together, sew across top, turn and press. Baste or pin around sides and bottom, sew to back lining just outside seam line. Assemble lining. Turn right side out and press.

6. (Optional) Place finished pocket on back lining, matching "X" on the pattern. Sew pocket to right side of back lining. Set aside.

7. Following manufacturer's instructions, attach the magnetic snap, matching the "X" on the purse front with the bag flap. Reinforce the area on purse front and flap lining with a 3" square of fusible interfacing. *Note: If using a regular snap, wait until purse construction is completed to add the snap.*

8. With right sides together, sew purse flap and flap lining together, leaving straight edge of flap open. Turn right side out and if you want a flat braid around the flap, sew it in place around the curved portion of the flap. *Note: If this is too thick for your machine, stitch in place by hand after purse is assembled.*

9. Make the strap as described below, then place the strap ends on the side seams inside the bag and sew in place.

   Flat fabric strap: Fold fabric in half lengthwise. Sew along outside edge and press seam open. *Note: Sew across one end of strap, this makes turning easier and then you can snip this sewn end off after it is turned.* Turn and press flat with seam in center along bottom of strap.

   Flat fabric strap with suede cloth underside: Turn under 1" on both sides of fabric and on both sides of suede cloth, then press. Place wrong sides together and edge-stitch with fabric on top and suede on bottom.

   Rolled strap: Fold bias fabric, right sides together, and sew around cotton cord, leaving 29" of cord uncovered in front of fabric (left end of cord). Sew across cord at beginning of fabric to secure cord in place. Pull right end of cord, pushing fabric over left part of cord. *Note: The fabric will now be right side out when it is reversed and it will cover up the left side of the cord. Cut off exposed right side of cord.*

10. Turn in ½" seam allowance on bag and lining and either slip-stitch or topstitch along edge with sewing machine.

11. Center flap on back of bag and sew in place.

12. Slip bag inside lining with right sides together. Sew around top of bag, leaving open between marks on top edge of pattern. Turn to right side, pushing lining into bag.

13. Adhere embellishments. See specific embellishment suggestions on the project page and the photograph of the bag you are making.

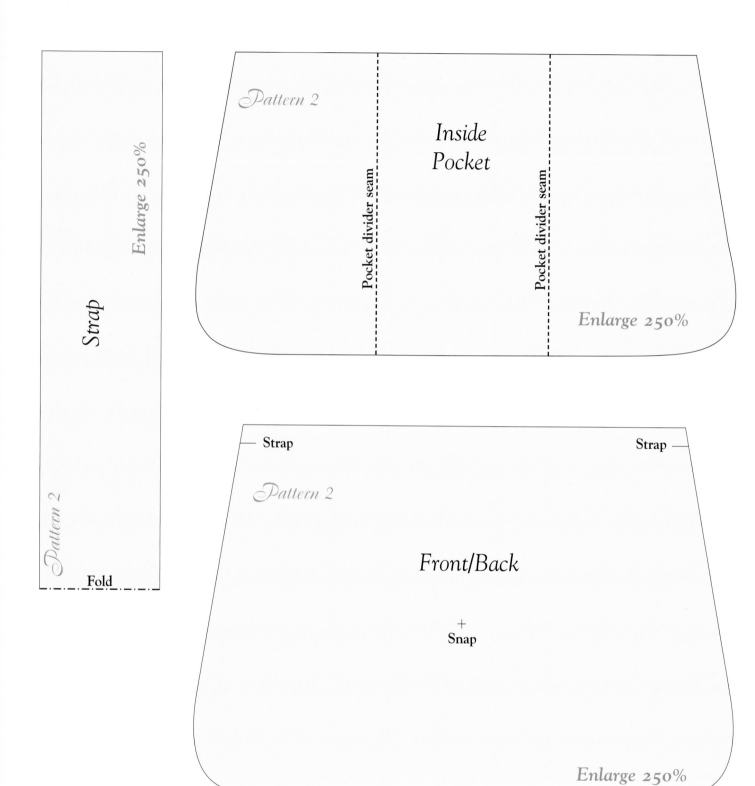

Enlarge 250%

Strap

Pattern 2

Fold

Pattern 2

Inside
Pocket

Pocket divider seam

Pocket divider seam

Enlarge 250%

Strap

Strap

Pattern 2

Front/Back

+
Snap

Enlarge 250%

Pattern 3

Finished size is 8" x 7" x 2½"—not counting trim. Pattern assumes ½" seam allowances included in the pattern and seams are pressed open.

Materials

Note: This list is appropriate for a generic version of the pattern. See Materials and Embellishments lists that accompany the titled purse to make the specific design shown.

- Basic fabric (¼ yd) for purse (⅜ yd if making a flat strap)
- Cord or chain (1¼ yds) for strap
- Flat braid trim, ¼"-wide (17") for flat strap with braid trim
- Fusible interfacing (⅙ yd) for flap
- Fusible medium-weight fleece** (¼ yd)
- Glues: fabric; industrial-strength
- Lining fabric (¼ yd)
- Magnetic snap or large regular snap
- Suede cloth, 2" x 17" for flat strap lining

** Fusible fleece is not necessary if your basic fabric is heavy-weight.

Preparation

1. Cut two pieces each of Front/Back pattern on page 106 from basic fabric, fusible fleece, and lining fabric.

2. Cut one piece each of Flap pattern on page 106 from basic fabric, fusible interfacing, and lining fabric.

3. Flat strap backed with suede cloth: Cut one piece of Strap pattern on page 106 from basic fabric.

Construction

1. Following manufacturer's directions, fuse fleece to wrong side of basic fabric front, back, and flap. *Note: Use fleece in all silk and medium fabric purses. Use interfacing in flaps. Do not use interfacing in body of heavier weight fabrics.*

2. With right sides together, sew front and back of bag together, leaving top open, and turn. *Note: Fringe or trim will now be around outside edge of sides and bottom.*

3. (Optional) Arrange embellishments you have chosen for the flap that require stitching in place on the right side of the flap and stitch. *Note: If embellishments are to be glued in place, wait until the purse is constructed.*

4. (Optional) If you are using fringe around the flap, place the heading of the fringe along the outside edge of the flap with the bottom of the fringe toward the center of the flap. Sew in place.

5. Following manufacturer's instructions, attach magnetic snap, matching "X" on purse front with bag flap. Reinforce area on purse front and flap lining with a 3"-square of fusible interfacing. *Note: If using a regular snap, wait until purse construction is completed to add snap.*

6. With right sides together, sew purse flap and flap lining together, leaving straight edge of flap open. Turn right side out and if you want a flat braid around the flap, sew it in place around the curved portion of the flap.

7. Make flat strap by turning under ½" on both sides of fabric and on both sides of suede cloth, then press. Place wrong sides together and edge-stitch with fabric on top and suede on bottom. Center and sew flat braid along length of strap. Place the strap ends or cord or chain ends on side seams inside bag. Hand-stitch in place.

8. Center flap on back of bag. Sew in place.

9. Slip bag inside lining with right sides together. Sew around top of bag, leaving open between marks on top edge of pattern. Turn to right side, pushing lining into bag.

10. Turn in ½" seam allowance of bag and lining and either slip-stitch or topstitch along edge with sewing machine.

11. Adhere embellishments. See specific embellishment suggestions on the project page and the photograph of the bag you are making.

Pattern 3

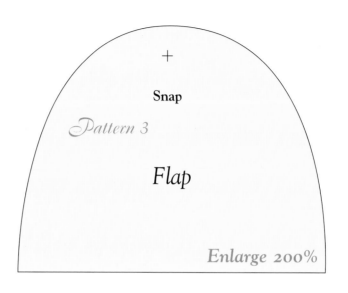

+

Snap

Pattern 3

Flap

Enlarge 200%

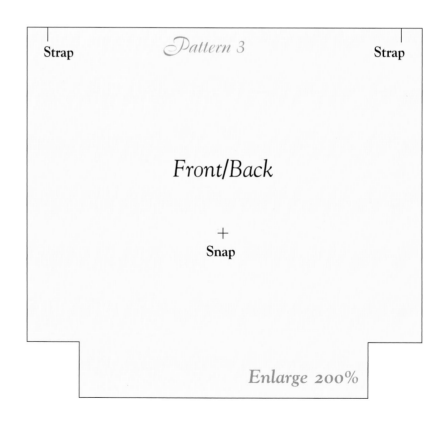

Strap   *Pattern 3*   **Strap**

Front/Back

+

Snap

Enlarge 200%

Pattern 4

Finished size is 14" x 13"—not counting trim. Pattern assumes ½" seam allowances included in the pattern.

Materials

Note: This list is appropriate for a generic version of the pattern. See Materials and Embellishments lists that accompany the titled purse to make the specific design shown.

- Basic fabric (¾ yd)
- Fusible fleece (light or medium weight)** (⅔ yd)
- Fusible interfacing (⅓ yd) for flap
- Lining fabric (⅔ yd)
- Looped fringe, ½"-wide (4⅛ yds)
- Magnetic snap
- Suede cloth, 3" x 30"

** Fusible fleece is not necessary if your basic fabric is heavy-weight.

Preparation

1. Cut one piece each of Back pattern below from basic fabric, fusible fleece, and lining fabric.

2. Cut one piece each of Front pattern on page 108 from basic fabric, fusible fleece, and lining fabric.

3. Cut one piece each of Flap pattern below from basic fabric, fusible interfacing, and lining fabric.

4. Flat strap backed with suede cloth: Cut one piece of Strap pattern on page 108 from basic fabric.

5. Cut two 3" x 3" squares from fusible interfacing to reinforce areas around magnetic snap.

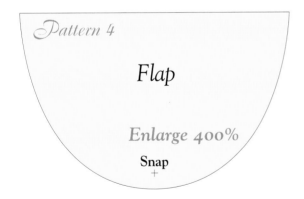

Pattern 4

Flap

Enlarge 400%

Snap
+

Pattern 4

Back

Enlarge 400%

Construction

1. Following manufacturer's directions, fuse fleece to wrong side of basic fabric front and back. *Note: Fuse fleece to lining, if you prefer.* Fuse interfacing to wrong side of flap. *Note: Use fleece in all silk and medium fabric purses. Use interfacing in flaps. Do not use interfacing in body of heavier weight fabrics.*

2. (Optional) Sew three rows of looped fringe or other trim to right side of bag front. The fringe header should be placed along outside edge of bag front with bottom of fringe toward center of piece and sewn in place. If you are using a contrasting color for the middle row of fringe, sandwich it between the other two rows of fringe. *Note: Do not remove manufacturer's stabilizing thread along bottom of fringe until fringe is sewn in place.*

3. With right sides together, sew front and back together, leaving top open. Turn right side out so fringe is now around the outside edge of sides and bottom of purse.

4. (Optional) On right side of flap fabric, arrange any embellishments you have chosen for the flap that require stitching. Stitch in place. *Note: If embellishments are to be glued or hand-stitched in place, wait until flap is completed.* Sew fringe or trim around the flap, using same method as for purse body in Step 2.

5. Reinforce area on purse front and flap lining for magnetic snap with a 3" square of fused interfacing. Following manufacturer's instructions, attach magnetic snap, matching the "X" on purse front with bag flap. If using a regular snap, sew in place after purse is assembled.

6. With right sides together, sew purse flap and flap lining together, leaving straight edge of flap open. Turn right side out and if you want a flat braid around flap, sew it in place around curved portion of flap. *Note: If this is too thick for your machine, stitch in place by hand after purse is assembled.*

7. Make flat strap by turning under 1" on both sides of fabric and on both sides of suede cloth, then press. Place wrong sides together and edge-stitch with fabric on top and suede on bottom. Place strap ends on side seams inside bag and sew in place.

8. Center flap on back of bag and sew in place.

9. Slip bag inside lining with right sides together. Sew around top of bag leaving open between marks on top edge of pattern. Turn to right side, pushing lining into bag.

10. Turn in ½" seam allowance of bag and lining and either slip-stitch or topstitch along edge with sewing machine. If using a regular snap, stitch onto flap and bag at this time.

11. Adhere embellishments. See specific embellishment suggestions on the project page and the photograph of the bag you are making.

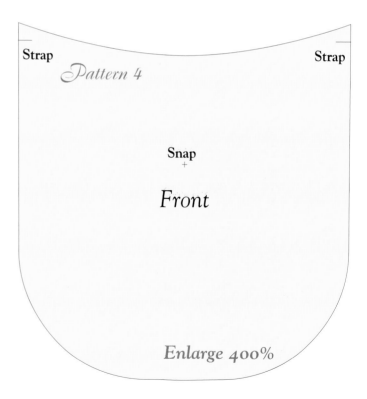

Strap *Pattern 4* **Strap**

Snap
+

Front

Enlarge 400%

Pattern 4 *Strap* Enlarge 400%

Pattern 5

Finished size is 14" x 12" x 3". Pattern assumes ½" seam allowances included in the pattern and seams are pressed open.

Materials

See Materials and Embellishments lists for Family Album on pages 18–19.

Preparation

1. If you are not a quilter, use this method of creating a crazy quilt to create the basic fabric in this design. *Note: If you are experienced in making crazy quilts, you may want to use another method.*

2. Make two copies each of Front, Back, and Flap patterns on pages 110–111 on paper. Each pattern piece will have multiple numbered crazy-quilt pieces. Cut out all of the pieces from one set to use as patterns. Keep pieces for pattern of front in an envelope labeled "Front" and do likewise for "Back" and "Flap."

3. Using second set of paper patterns, cut one each of Front, Back, and Flap patterns from cotton muslin, fusible fleece, and lining fabric. Place muslin on top of these pattern pieces and mark piece number and outlines on muslin with fabric tracing paper. *Note: These lines will not show once the bag is finished.* Set other fabric pieces aside.

4. Using cut-out paper pattern pieces, cut one each from silk and velvet fabrics, leaving ½" seam allowance on each piece, except on outside seams where the ½" is included. As you cut out each piece, leave pattern piece pinned to fabric. Match each piece to corresponding space on the muslin pattern.

5. Cut two 3" x 3" squares from fusible interfacing to reinforce areas around magnetic snap.

Crazy-quilt Pieces

1. **To Stitch:** Remove a few pieces pinned to the muslin and set aside. Start in upper-left corner with piece #1 and machine-sew in place. Match seams with #2, right sides together, sew and press flat. Continue across top row. Where you can't seam on the wrong side, fold under seam allowances and do one of the following options: a) machine-sew, b) slip-stitch, or c) baste and do an embroidery stitch to hold in place.

2. **Back:** Sew around heart-shaped piece just inside the seam line. Clip and press seam to wrong side. Sew ruffled trim around the heart. Set aside. Sew all other pieces in place, using the method in Step 1. Appliqué finished heart piece to center of back. *Note: This can be done on the sewing machine. Stitches will be covered with the blue/green silk flower trim.*

3. **Front and Flap:** Follow same method used in Step 1.

4. After all pattern pieces have been pieced, proceed with the trims. Hand-stitch silk flower trims along desired seams, machine- or hand-embroider along remaining seams, except short seams where flower trim sections will be placed.

5. Place silk lady prints in desired locations and stitch. Frame one with beaded velvet trim by hand-stitching; make loops at top and sew three pearls in loops to form a bouquet. Frame second print with purple/green silk flower trim by hand-stitching; stitch a cluster of flowers at the top and add two pearls.

6. Hand-stitch flower trim sections along short seams.

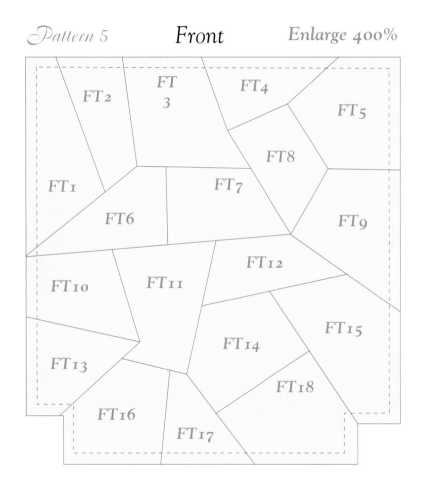

Pattern 5 Front *Enlarge 400%*

FT2
FT3
FT4
FT5
FT8
FT1
FT7
FT6
FT9
FT10
FT11
FT12
FT15
FT13
FT14
FT18
FT16
FT17

Construction

1. Following manufacturer's directions, fuse front, back, and flap fleece pieces to wrong sides of corresponding lining pieces.

2. With right sides together, sew bottom seam and press. Sew side seams. Bring side and bottom seams together and sew to form bottom.

3. (Optional) Arrange embellishments for the flap that require stitching in place on the right side of the flap and stitch. *Note: If embellishments are to be glued in place, wait until the purse is constructed.* To stitch looped fringe around the flap, place the heading of the fringe along the outside edge of the flap with the bottom of the fringe toward the center of the flap. Sew in place.

4. Following manufacturer's instructions, attach magnetic snap, matching the purse front with the inside of the bag flap. Reinforce area on purse front and flap lining with a 3" square of fusible interfacing. *Note: If using a regular snap, wait until purse is constructed to add snap.*

5. With right sides together, sew purse flap and flap lining together, leaving straight edge of the flap open. Turn right side out.

6. To make strap, fold each side of the suede cloth ¾" toward the center and overlap. Lay flat trim on the top and sew down each side of the trim.

7. Place strap ends on side seams with right sides facing outside of strap. Sew in place.

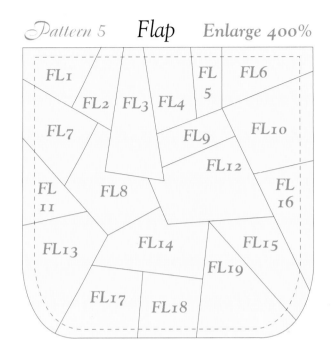

8. Center flap on back of bag and sew in place.

9. Slip bag inside lining with right sides together. Sew around top of bag, leaving an opening for turning on top front edge of pattern. Turn to right side, pushing lining into bag.

10. Turn in ½" seam allowance around top of bag and lining. Slip-stitch or topstitch along edge with sewing machine.

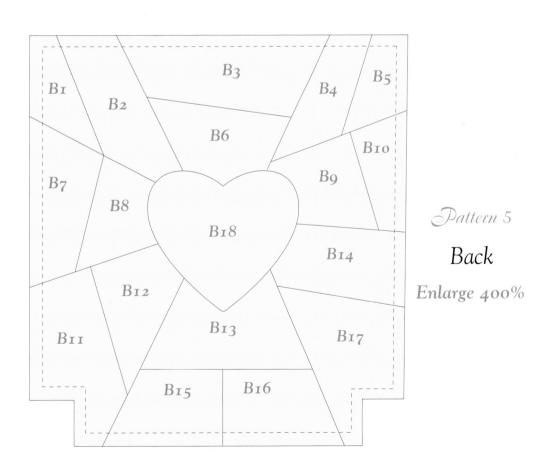

Pattern 5

Back

Enlarge 400%

Pattern 6

This pattern is used to construct the following purse:
Vanity Fair

Pattern assumes ½" seam allowances included in the pattern and seams are pressed open.

Materials

Note: This list is appropriate for a generic version of the pattern. See Materials and Embellishments lists that accompany the titled purse to make the specific design shown.

- Basic fabric (⅜ yd)
- Lining fabric (¼ yd)
- Looped fringe: main color, ½"-wide (1⅓ yds); contrasting color, ½"-wide (⅔ yd)
- Rhinestones (12)
- Zipper, 7"

Preparation

1. Cut two each of Front/Back pattern on page 113 from basic fabric and lining fabric.
2. Cut one of Wrist Strap pattern (13" x 2½") on page 113 from basic fabric.
3. Cut one of Loop Strap pattern (3½" x 2½") on page 113 from basic fabric.

Construction

1. Fold in strap and loop seam allowances to wrong side and press. Fold strap and loop in half, matching folded edges. Topstitch close to edge.
2. Pin strap ends to purse front between marks. Repeat process with the loop. Sew both just inside seam line.
3. Place front and back pieces, right sides together, and sew along top, leaving opening for zipper. Press seam open and insert zipper, following package instructions.
4. Sew three rows of looped fringe, with contrast in the middle, around purse body front.
5. Unzip zipper. With right sides together, sew seam around body, being careful not to catch loops in seam. Trim seam.
6. Place lining front and back, right sides together, and sew along top, leaving opening for zipper. Press seam open.
7. With right sides together, stitch around body of the lining. Turn right side out.
8. Slip purse inside lining, with wrong sides together, and either hand-stitch lining to zipper or sew along purse stitching.
9. Turn lining inside purse.
10. Apply rhinestones to wrist strap—five on front and five on back—and one on each side of loop.

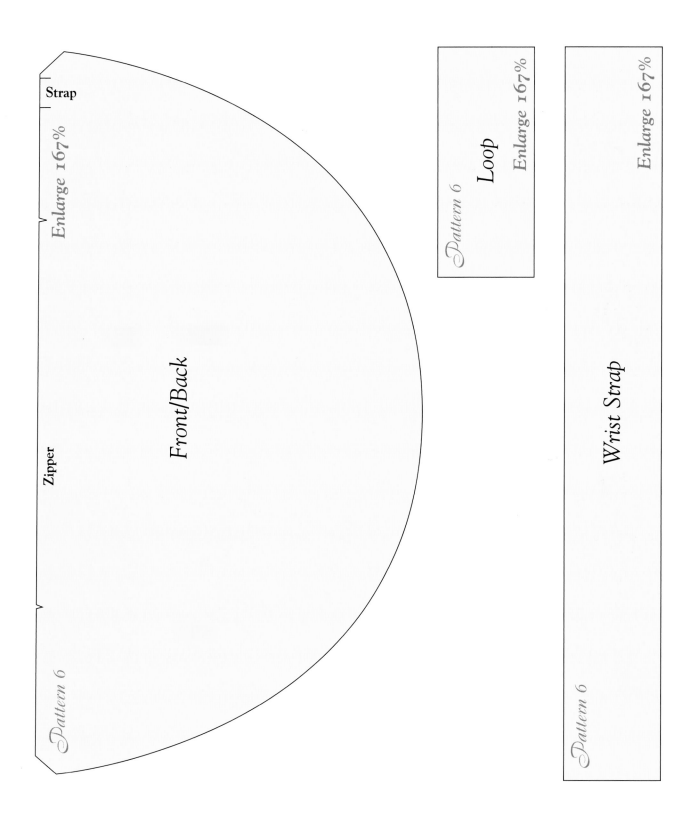

Strap

Enlarge 167%

Zipper

Front/Back

Pattern 6

Pattern 6

Loop

Enlarge 167%

Enlarge 167%

Wrist Strap

Pattern 6

Pattern 7

Finished size is 8" x 11½". Pattern assumes ½" seam allowances included in the pattern and seams are pressed open.

Materials

See Materials and Embellishments lists for Apple Blossom on page 56.

Preparation

1. Cut two each of Front/Back and Gusset patterns below and on page 115, and six 3" x 24" ruffles from embroidered silk.

2. Cut two each of Gusset and Lining patterns below and on page 115 from lining fabric and fusible fleece.

Construction

1. Sew ruffled trim to the bottom of each ruffle piece. Press trim header toward ruffle and sew to finish bottom edge.

2. Fold in top of ruffle and press. Sew one gathering row ¼" from fold and another gathering row close to first. Gather and sew along stitching lines marked on pattern pieces for purse front and back.

3. With right sides together, sew gusset into each side of purse, sewing ruffle ends into seams. Sew from bottom of gusset along bottom seam line to bottom of gusset on other side.

4. Fuse fleece pieces to wrong side of lining pieces.

5. With right sides together, sew lining gusset into each side of lining. Sew from bottom of gusset along bottom seam line to bottom of gusset on other side.

6. Slip purse into lining, with right sides together; sew top of gusset and along sides of purse top, leaving top open. Turn and push lining to inside of purse.

7. Fold top on seam line shown on pattern pieces and sew along seam line. Sew along second seam line to form a channel for purse frame bar.

8. Hand-stitch acrylic chokers or other bead embellishments along top of front and back ruffle seam lines.

9. Remove cap from one end of frame bar. Slip bar into ring on frame and into purse channel. Slip bar into ring on opposite side of frame. Screw cap onto bar to hold it in place.

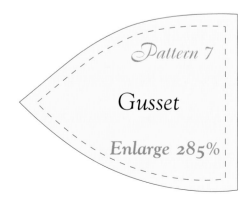

Pattern 7

Gusset

Enlarge 285%

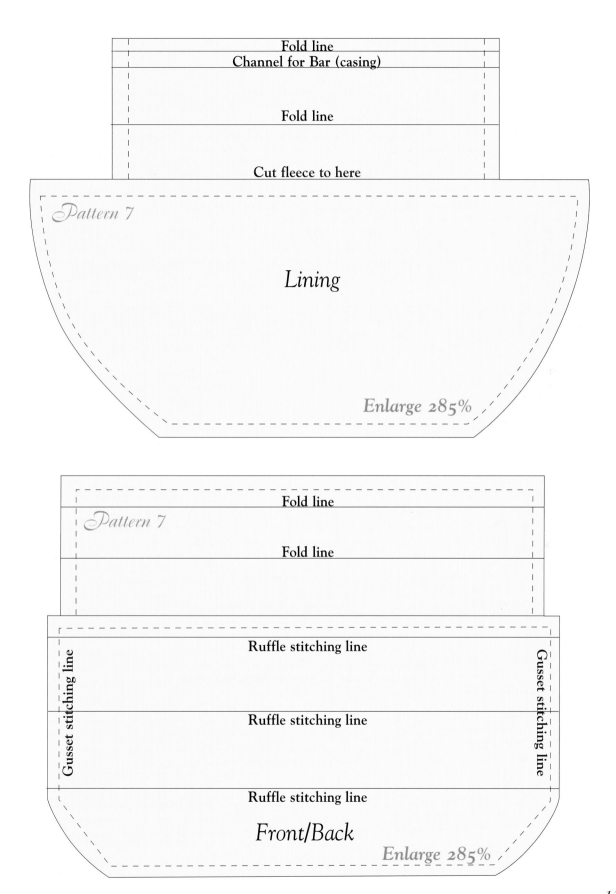

Fold line

Channel for Bar (casing)

Fold line

Cut fleece to here

Pattern 7

Lining

Enlarge 285%

Fold line

Pattern 7

Fold line

Gusset stitching line

Ruffle stitching line

Gusset stitching line

Ruffle stitching line

Ruffle stitching line

Front/Back

Enlarge 285%

Pattern 8

This pattern is used to construct the following purses:
Madame Marie • Mon Cheri!

Pattern assumes ½" seam allowances included in the pattern.

Materials

Note: This list is appropriate for a generic version of the pattern. See Materials and Embellishments lists that accompany the titled purse to make the specific design shown.

- Basic fabric (⅔ yd)
- Bead drop fringe, ½"-wide (1 yd)
- Contrasting velvet (½ yd)
- Cord, ⅛" dia. (20")
- Fancy fringe (same color as velvet), ½"-wide (2 yds)
- Flat trim (same color as velvet) (2 yds)
- Fusible fleece (⅔ yd)
- Industrial-strength glue
- Large shank button
- Lining fabric (⅔ yd)
- Metallic or fancy cord, ¼" dia. (3½ yds)
- Safety pin

Preparation

1. Cut one piece each of Body pattern on page 117 from basic fabric, velvet, lining fabric, and fusible fleece.

2. Cut one piece of Bottom pattern on page 117 from velvet.

3. Cut one piece each of Circle pattern on page 117 from lining fabric and fusible fleece.

Construction

1. With right sides together, sew basic fabric body piece along 13" edge. Press and set aside.

2. With right sides together, stitch velvet bottom piece along 6" edge. Press and turn to right side.

3. Turn under 1" along bottom of velvet bottom piece and sew ½" from folded edge, leaving ¾" opening on seam line. *Note: This forms a casing for cord.*

4. With right sides together, sew basic fabric body piece and raw edge of velvet bottom piece together. Turn to right side and press.

5. Stitch fancy fringe along bottom and top edges of basic fabric body.

6. Attach safety pin to end of 20" cord and run it through the casing on the velvet for bottom of purse. Pull it as tightly as possible and tie securely. Trim off excess cord and push ends inside purse. With industrial-strength glue, glue large shank button over hole on outside of velvet bottom. When glue is dry, stitch it with strong thread through shank from inside of purse.

7. Fuse fleece to lining body and lining circle.

8. With right sides together sew lining body piece along 13" edge. Sew around bottom, just inside seam line. Then, with right sides together, sew lining bottom to lining body.

9. With wrong sides together, sew lining and purse body together along top edge. Push lining down into purse.

10. You are now ready to add the velvet top. With right sides of the top velvet together, sew ½" seam allowance along the 13" edge, leaving a ¾" opening ¾" from fold line, which is 6½" from the edge.

11. Fold top piece of velvet in half, wrong sides together and sew 1¼" from fold and again ¾" from fold. This will form a casing for the fancy drawstring cord.

12. With right sides together, sew body of purse and lining to 32" side of velvet, leaving inside velvet free. *Note: This will become the lining of the outside velvet.*

13. Sew beaded fringe along top of fancy fringe around top of purse.

14. Press and fold in seam of velvet lining, then slip-stitch along the seam line.

15. Glue flat trim along top of fancy fringe around top and bottom of the purse.

16. Attach safety pin to a 30" piece of fancy cord and run it through casing at top of bag. Knot ends of cord together. Stitch ornamental beads onto knots. Finish off ends with tiny beads. Stitch a few times and secure with industrial glue.

17. To make strap, cut one 38" piece from fancy cord. String one of the embellishment dangles on the cord and stitch in place on side of purse, leaving an area open to get glue under the coil. Repeat on other side.

18. With remaining cord, make another coil and stitch and glue to the first coil and twist it around the first coil tightly, then take the cord around the purse to the other coil. Repeat with a coil around the second side, stitch and glue. Glue ½" antique button in center of each coil.

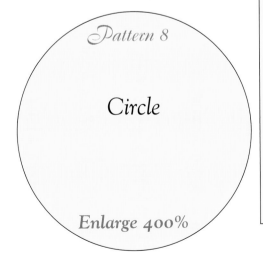

Pattern 8

Circle

Enlarge 400%

Pattern 8

Bottom

Enlarge 400%

Pattern 8

Body

Enlarge 400%

Pattern 9

Finished size is 8" x 9"—not counting last row of fringe. This purse pattern is a simple rectangle, no patterns are needed.

Materials

Note: This list is appropriate for a generic version of the pattern. See Materials and Embellishments lists that accompany the titled purse to make the specific design shown.

- Bas relief lady's profile
- Basic fabric (⅓ yd)
- Chain to match purse frame (39")
- Complimentary lining fabric (⅓ yd)
- Glues: fabric; industrial-strength
- Hem tape matching basic fabric (½ yd)
- Metallic leaves
- Purse frame with rod, 5"-wide
- Silky fringe, ½"-wide (1 yd)
- Small feathers
- Velvet leaves

Preparation

1. Cut basic fabric to 11" x 18".
2. Cut lining fabric to 11" x 18".
3. Cut fusible fleece to 8½" x 18".

Construction

This purse has only one vertical seam. It is in the center back. There will be slits at the top on both sides of the purse to allow the purse frame to open properly.

1. Fuse fleece to basic fabric along 18" edge. *Note: This will leave 3½" at the top.*

2. Place header of bottom row of fringe about ⅜" above bottom of basic fabric, right sides together. Sew it where you are catching only about ⅛" of fringe header. *Note: The purpose is to stitch to bottom row of fringe into the bottom seam (see Step 7).*

3. Place second row of fringe right side up on basic fabric. Sew second row of fringe so loops fall ¼" over bottom fringe header.

4. With right sides together, pin lining to basic fabric. Find center of fabric pieces and make a mark. *Note: This will become center front of purse.* To make slits for purse rods on either side, measure 4¼" from center on both sides and mark. At side marks, draw vertical 5" lines starting at top edge.

5. Sew lining and basic fabric ¼" from lines on both sides, tapering at the bottom. Reinforce stitching at bottom of lines. Cut along lines, clipping close to bottom point. Turn and press.

6. With right sides of basic fabric together, sew back seam. Press seam open. Repeat with lining.

7. With right sides together, match back seam to center front mark and sew along bottom seam line of basic fabric with ⅛" of fringe header inside the seam. Repeat with lining. Trim seams and turn purse and lining to right side, push lining to inside of purse.

8. On both front and back pieces at top of purse, sew hem tape along purse and lining top, leaving ½" of hem tape on each end. Fold in the four ½" seam tape pieces and sew. Fold the top of the purse to the inside 1½" (including the seam tape). Sew close to hem tape edge and sew again ½" from seam line to form casing for purse frame rod.

9. Adhere embellishments. See specific embellishment suggestions on the project page and the photograph of the bag you are making.

10. Unscrew cap from purse frame rod. Run rod though front purse frame ring, through casing, and through frame ring on other side. Screw on cap and repeat on back side of purse.

11. Attach chain to purse frame rings.

Pattern 10

Finished size is 12" x 10" x 3"—not including trim. Pattern assumes ½" seam allowances included in the pattern and seams are pressed open.

Materials

Note: This list is appropriate for a generic version of the pattern. See Materials and Embellishments lists that accompany the titled purse to make the specific design shown.

- Contrasting fabric (⅙ yd) for piping
- Cording (1¼ yds) for strap or chain (1¼ yds)
- Fabric of choice (½ yd) for purse
- Glues: fabric; industrial-strength
- Fusible fleece medium weight ** (½ yd)
- Fusible interfacing (⅙ yd) for flap
- Lining fabric (½ yd)
- Magnetic snap or large regular snap

** Fusible fleece is not necessary if your basic fabric is heavy-weight.

Preparation

1. Cut two each of Front/Back pattern on page 120 from basic fabric, fusible fleece, lining fabric.

2. Cut one each of Flap pattern on page 120 from basic fabric, lining fabric, and fusible interfacing.

3. Cut contrasting fabric for piping 1½" x 63" (this may be done in sections, each the length of sides, bottom, and flap.) Cut the cord to the same lengths. Cover the cord with the contrasting fabric and sew close to the cord, using a zipper foot. Set aside.

Construction

1. Following manufacturer's directions, fuse the fleece to the wrong side of lining front and back. Fuse interfacing to wrong side of lining of flap. *Note: Use fleece in all silk and medium fabric purse. Only use interfacing in the flaps and none in the body of heavier weight fabrics. Fuse fleece to lining pieces when the body fabric is heavy. When using lighter fabric, fuse it to the basic fabric.*

2. If you are using contrasting piping, looped fringe or fringe with a plain header sew around the body fabric flap, right sides together. Arrange the embellishments you have chosen for the flap that require stitching on place on the right side of the flap and stitch. *Note: If embellishments are to be glued in place, wait until purse is constructed.*

3. With right sides together, sew front and back of bag together along bottom edge, press seam open. Stitch side edges and press seam open. Match side and bottom seams together and stitch a seam to form the bottom. Leave top open and turn.

4. Following manufacturer's instructions, attach magnetic snap, matching the "X" on the purse front with the bag flap. Reinforce the area on purse front and flap lining with a 3" square of fused interfacing. *Note: If using a regular snap, wait until purse construction is completed to add snap.*

5. With right sides together, sew purse flap and flap lining together, leaving straight edge of flap open. Turn right side out and, if you want a flat braid around the flap, sew in place around the curved portion of the flap.

6. Place strap or cord on the side seams inside the bag and hand-stitch in place.

7. Center flap on back of bag and sew in place.

8. Slip bag inside lining with right sides together. Sew around top of bag leaving open between marks on top edge of pattern. Turn to right side, pushing lining into bag.

9. Turn in ½" seam of bag and lining and sew with either a slip-stitch or topstitch along edge .

10. Adhere remaining embellishments. See specific embellishment suggestions on the project page and the photograph of the bag you are making.

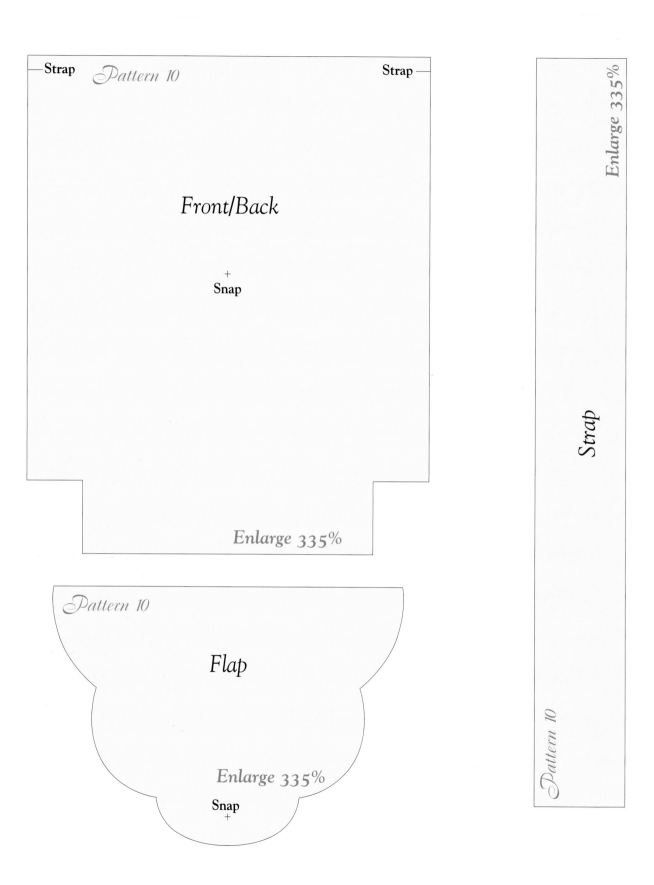

Strap *Pattern 10* **Strap**

Enlarge 335%

Front/Back

+
Snap

Enlarge 335%

Strap

Pattern 10

Flap

Enlarge 335%

Snap
+

Pattern 10

120

Pattern II

Finished size is 11½" x 8" x 3". Pattern assumes ½" seam allowances included in the pattern and seams are pressed open.

Materials

Note: This list is appropriate for a generic version of the pattern. See Materials and Embellishments lists that accompany the titled purse to make the specific design shown.

- Basic fabric (⅔ yd)
- Contrasting fabric (⅓ yd)
- Fringe in third color, 1"-wide (¾ yd per row) (optional)
- Fusible fleece (⅓ yd)
- Fusible interfacing (3"-wide strip)
- Lining fabric (⅓ yd)

Preparation

1. Cut two each of Front/Back pattern on page 122 from basic fabric and lining fabric.
2. Cut one of Cuff pattern on page 122 on a fold from contrasting fabric.
3. Cut two of Lining pattern on page 122 from lining fabric and fusible fleece.
4. Cut one 3" piece of interfacing as long as the cuff piece.
5. Cut one of Strap pattern (3½" x 25") on page 122 from contrasting fabric.

Construction

1. With right sides together, sew bottom edge of purse body and press seam open.
2. Sew purse body side edgess and press seams open.
3. Bring body side seams and bottom seam together; sew across to form ends of purse bottom.
4. With right sides together, sew fringe around top of cuff in contrasting fabric. Set aside. Sew back seam of cuff and press open.
5. Fuse 3" piece of fusible interfacing to inside of cuff, over marks for snaps.
6. With right sides together, sew cuff over flat trim and body, this will insert the trim into the seam. Turn and press seam edge.
7. Insert magnetic snap on marks indicted on pattern.
8. Fuse fleece to lining and follow same method used for making body of purse.
9. With right sides together, sew fleeced-lined lining to cuff, leaving 8" opening. Pull purse and lining to right side through 8" opening. Push lining into purse. Hand-stitch opening securely with strong thread.
10. Fold strap edges to inside ¾" on each side and press. Lay flat trim on top of raw edges and stew close to edges on each side of trim.
11. Sew strap on each side seam, 2½" from cuff and fringe seam line, with underside of strap laying with raw edge down toward stitching line. Turn down cuff to outside of purse.
12. Sew and glue buttons to cover strap stitching. Embellish with millinery corsage or vintage brooch.

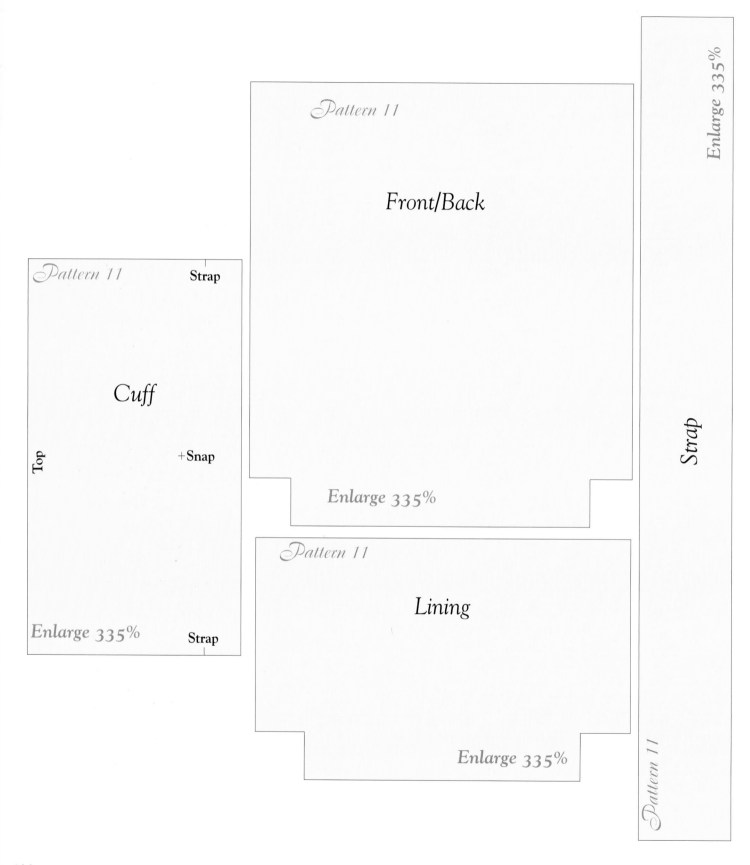

Pattern 11

Front/Back

Enlarge 335%

Pattern 11   **Strap**

Cuff

Top   **+Snap**

Enlarge 335%   **Strap**

Pattern 11

Lining

Enlarge 335%

Enlarge 335%

Strap

Pattern 11

Pattern 12

Finished size is 9" x 13" x 3"—not counting trim. Pattern assumes ½" seam allowances included in the pattern and seams are pressed open.

Materials

Note: This list is appropriate for a generic version of the pattern. See Materials and Embellishments lists that accompany the titled purse to make the specific design shown.

- Basic fabric (¾ yd) or (⅞ yd) if making a flat strap
- Cotton piping ½" dia., (2 yds) for rolled strap
- Flat braid trim (30") for flat strap with braid trim
- Fusible interfacing (¼ yd) for flap
- Fusible medium-weight fleece** (½ yd)
- Lining fabric (½ yd)
- Rayon looped fringe, ½"-wide (4⅛ yds)
- Suede cloth, 3" x 30" for flat strap lining

** Fusible fleece is not necessary if your basic fabric is heavy-weight.

Preparation

1. Cut two each of Front/Back pattern on page 125 from basic fabric, lining fabric, and fusible fleece or fusible interfacing according to the weight of your fabric. (See Step 1 in Construction.)

2. Cut one each of Gusset pattern on page 125 on the fold from basic fabric, lining fabric, and fusible fleece.

3. Cut one each of Flap pattern on page 124 from basic fabric, lining fabric, and fusible interfacing or fleece.

4. Cut two 3" squares of interfacing to reinforce the area of the snap on flap and body.

5. **Flat strap:** Cut one 4" x 30" piece of both basic fabric and interfacing for 1½" x 39" strap.

   Flat strap with braid trim: Cut a 30" piece of flat braid to trim fabric strap.

   Rolled strap: Cut a 3" x 30" piece of fabric on bias and a piece of ½"-dia. cotton piping that is double the length of the finished strap length.

   Flat strap backed with suede cloth: Cut a 3" x 30" piece from both basic fabric and suede cloth.

Construction

1. Following manufacturer's directions, fuse interfacing fleece to wrong side of basic fabric front and back. Fuse interfacing to basic fabric or lining for flap. *Note: Use fleece in all silk and medium fabric purses. Use interfacing in flaps and not in the body of heavier weight fabrics.*

2. (Optional) Sew looped fringe or other trim to the right side of the bag front. The header of the fringe should be placed along the outside edge of the bag front with the bottom of the fringe toward the center of the piece. If you are using multiple rows of fringe, place the first color of fringe along the edge as described and second color on top of first row. *Note: Do not remove the manufacturer's stabilizing thread along the bottom of the fringe until the fringe is stitched in place.*

3. With right sides together, sew front and back of bag together leaving top open and turn. *Note: Fringe or trim will now be around the outside edge of sides and bottom of the purse.*

4. (Optional) Arrange embellishments you have chosen for the flap that require stitching in place on the right side of the flap and stitch. *Note: If embellishments are to be glued in place, wait until flap is completed.* Sew fringe or trim around flap using same method as for purse body.

5. Take two pocket pieces cut from lining fabric, with right sides together, stitch across top. Turn and press. Baste or pin around sides and bottom, sew to back lining–just outside seam line. Assemble lining. Place finished pocket on back lining, matching "X" on pattern. Sew pocket to right side of back lining. Set aside.

6. Following manufacturer's instructions, attach magnetic snap, matching "X" on purse front with bag flap. Reinforce area on purse front and flap lining with a 3" square of fused interfacing. *Note: If using a regular snap, wait until purse construction is completed to add snap.*

7. With right sides together, sew purse flap and flap lining together, leaving straight edge of flap open. Turn right side out. If you want a flat braid around the flap, sew it in place around the curved portion of the flap. *Note: If this is too thick for your machine, stitch in place by hand after purse is assembled.*

8. Make strap as described below and place strap ends on side seams inside bag and sew in place.

   Flat fabric strap: Fold fabric in half lengthwise. Sew along the outside edge, press the seam open. *Note: If you sew across one end of the strap, this makes turning easier and you can then snip this sewn end off after it has been turned.* After turning, press flat with the seam in the center along the bottom of the strap.

   Flat fabric strap with suede cloth underside: Turn under 1" on both sides of fabric and on both sides of suede cloth and press. Place wrong sides together and edge-stitch with fabric on top and suede on bottom.

Rolled strap: Fold bias fabric, right sides together, and sew around the cotton cord, leaving 29" of cord uncovered in front of the fabric (left end of cord). Sew across the cord at the beginning of the fabric to secure cord in place. Pull right end of the cord, pushing fabric over left part of cord. *Note: The fabric will be now be right side out when it is reversed and it will cover up the left side of the cord.* Cut off exposed right side of cord.

9. Center the flap on the back of the bag and sew in place.

10. Slip the bag inside the lining with right sides together. Sew around the top of the bag leaving open between the marks on top edge of the pattern. Turn to right side, pushing lining into bag.

11. Turn in ½" seam allowance of bag and lining and sew with either a slip-stitch or topstitch along edge.

12. Adhere remaining embellishments. See specific embellishment suggestions on the project page and the photograph of the bag you are making.

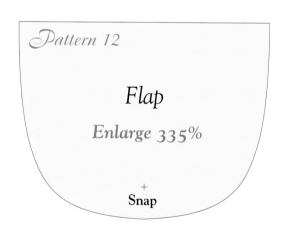

Pattern 12

Flap

Enlarge 335%

+

Snap

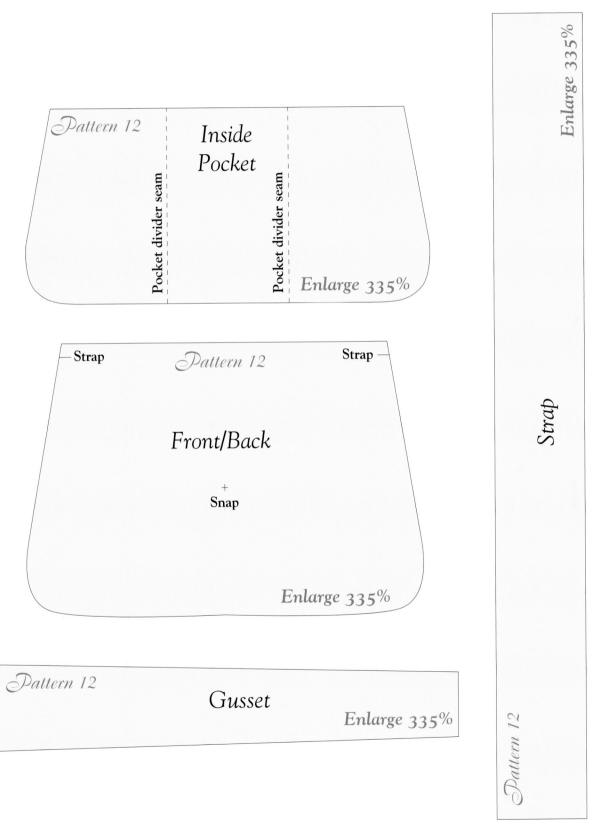

Pattern 12

Inside Pocket

Pocket divider seam

Pocket divider seam

Enlarge 335%

Strap *Pattern 12* **Strap**

Front/Back

+
Snap

Enlarge 335%

Pattern 12

Gusset

Enlarge 335%

Enlarge 335%

Strap

Pattern 12

Pattern 13

Finished size is 18½" x 12½" x 3"—not counting trim. Pattern assumes ½" seam allowances included in the pattern and seams are pressed open.

Materials

Note: This list is appropriate for a generic version of the pattern. See Materials and Embellishments lists that accompany the titled purse to make the specific design shown.

- Basic fabric, 45"-wide (1⅔ yds) or 60"-wide (1⅛ yds)
- Cotton piping, ½" dia. (2 yds) for rolled strap
- Flat braid trim, ¾"-wide (30") for flat fabric strap with braid trim
- Fusible medium-weight fleece** (½ yd)
- Fusible interfacing (¼ yd) for flap and snap
- Industrial-strength glue
- Lining fabric, 45"-wide (1⅔ yds)
- Magnetic snap
- Rayon looped, flat or ball fringe, 3"-wide (4⅔ yds) (optional)
- Suede cloth (3½" x 40") for flat strap lining

** Fusible fleece is not necessary if your basic fabric is heavy-weight.

Preparation

1. Cut two each of Front/Back pattern on page 128 from basic fabric, lining fabric, and fusible fleece or fusible interfacing according to the weight of your fabric. (See Step 1 in Construction.)

2. Cut one each of Gusset pattern on page 128 on the fold from basic fabric, lining fabric, and fleece.

3. Cut one each of Flap pattern on page 129 from basic fabric, lining fabric, and fusible interfacing or fleece.

4. (Optional) Cut two of Inside Pocket on page 129 from lining fabric.

5. Cut two 3"-square pieces of interfacing to reinforce the area of the snap on flap and body.

6. **Flat strap:** Cut one 3½" x 40" piece of both basic fabric and interfacing for 1½" x 39" strap.

   Flat strap with braid trim: Cut a 40" piece of flat braid to trim fabric strap.

   Rolled strap: Cut a 3½" x 40" piece of fabric on bias and a piece of ½" diameter cotton piping twice the length of the finished strap length.

   Flat strap backed with suede cloth: Cut a 3½" x 40" piece from both basic fabric and suede cloth .

Construction

1. Following manufacturer's directions, fuse interfacing or fleece to wrong side of basic fabric front and back. Fuse interfacing or fleece to the lining for the flap. *Note: Use fusible fleece in all silk and medium fabric purses. Use interfacing in the flaps and none in the body of heavier weight fabrics.*

2. (Optional) Sew fringe or other trim to the right side of the bag front and back. The header of the fringe should be placed along the outside edge of the bag front with the bottom of the fringe toward the center of the piece. If using multiple rows of fringe, place

first color of fringe along edge as described and second color on top of first row. *Note: If using looped fringe, do not remove the manufacturer's stabilizing thread along the bottom of the fringe until the fringe is stitched in place.*

3. With right sides together, sew front to one side of gusset; repeat for the back of bag. Leave top open and turn. *Note: Fringe or trim will now be around the outside edge of sides and bottom of the purse.*

4. (Optional) Arrange any embellishments you have chosen for the flap that require stitching in place on the right side of the flap and stitch. *Note: If embellishments are to be glued in place, wait until flap is completed.* Sew fringe or trim around the flap using the same method as for the purse body.

5. Take the two pocket pieces cut from lining fabric, with right sides together, sew across the top, down the sides and bottom, leaving a 3" opening to turn. After turning, slip-stitch and press. Place finished pocket on the back lining, matching "X" on pattern. Sew pocket to right side of back lining. Set aside.

6. Following manufacturer's instructions, attach magnetic snap, matching "X" on purse front with bag flap. Reinforce area on purse front and flap lining with a 3" square of fused interfacing. *Note: If using a regular snap, wait until purse construction is completed to add the snap.*

7. With right sides together, sew purse flap and flap lining together, leaving straight edge of flap open. Turn right side out and, if you want a flat braid around the flap, sew it in place around the curved portion of the flap. *Note: If too thick for your machine, stitch in place by hand after purse is assembled.*

8. Make strap as described below and place strap ends on side seams inside bag and sew in place.

   Flat one fabric strap: Fold fabric in half lengthwise. Sew along the outside edge and press the seam open. *Note: Sewing across one end of the strap makes turning easier and you can then snip this sewn end off after it has been turned.* After turning, press flat with the seam in the center along the bottom of the strap.

   Flat fabric strap with suede cloth underside: Turn under 1" on both sides of fabric and on both sides of suede cloth and press. Place wrong sides together and edge-stitch with fabric on top and suede on bottom.

   Rolled strap: Fold bias fabric, right sides together, and sew around the cotton cord, leaving 29" of cord uncovered in front of the fabric (left end of cord). Stitch across the cord at the beginning of the fabric to secure cord in place. Pull right end of cord, pushing fabric over left part of cord. *Note: The fabric will be now be right side out when it is reversed and it will cover up the left side of the cord.* Cut off exposed right side of cord.

9. Center flap on back of bag and sew in place.

10. Slip bag inside lining with right sides together. Sew around top of bag leaving open between marks on top edge of pattern. Turn to right side, pushing lining into bag.

11. Turn in ½" seam allowance of bag and lining and sew with either a slip-stitch or topstitch along edge.

12. Adhere remaining embellishments. See specific embellishment suggestions on the project page and the photograph of the bag you are making.

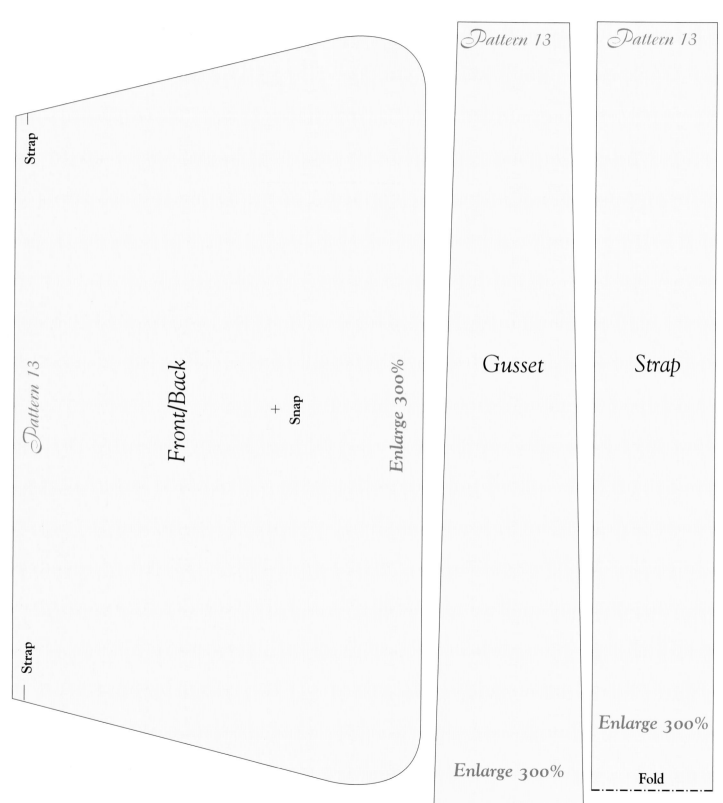

Strap

Pattern 13

Front/Back

+
Snap

Enlarge 300%

Strap

Pattern 13

Pattern 13

Gusset

Strap

Enlarge 300%

Enlarge 300%

Fold

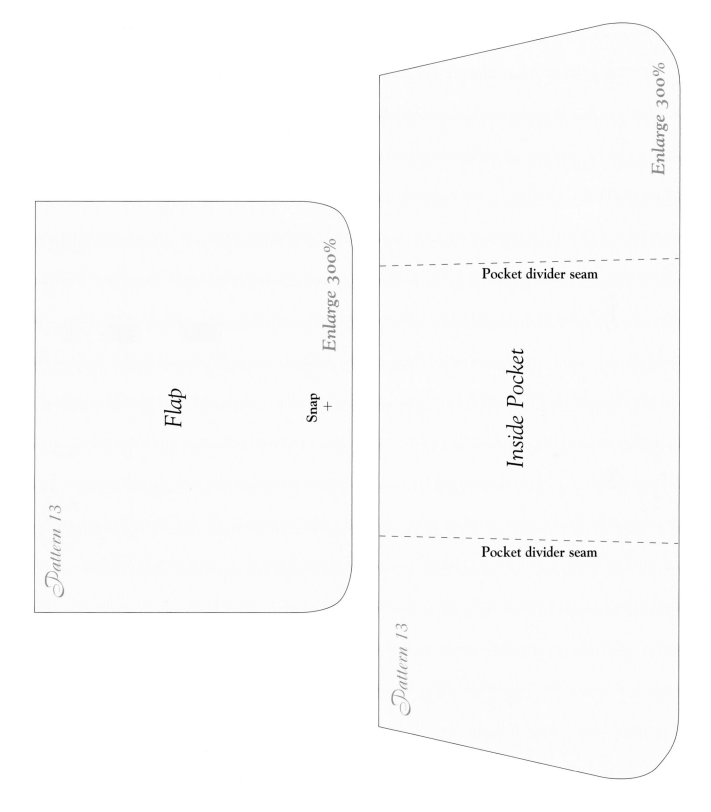

Pattern 13

Flap

Snap
+

Enlarge 300%

Enlarge 300%

Pocket divider seam

Inside Pocket

Pocket divider seam

Pattern 13

Pattern 14

Finished size is 9" x 12"—not counting trim. Pattern assumes ½" seam allowances included in the pattern and seams are pressed open.

Materials

Note: This list is appropriate for a generic version of the pattern. See Materials and Embellishments lists that accompany the titled purse to make the specific design shown.

- Basic fabric, 45"-wide (½ yd)
- Fusible fleece (⅓ yd)
- Industrial-strength glue
- Matching chain (39") (optional)
- Purse frame with rods, 6½"- or 7½"-wide
- Silk lining fabric, 45"-wide (½ yd)

Preparation

1. Cut two each of Front/Back pattern on page 131 from basic fabric and lining fabric.

2. Cut two of Front/Back pattern from fusible fleece to the uppermost stitching line.

3. Fuse fleece to wrong side of basic fabric pieces unless otherwise directed on design page.

Construction

1. (Optional) If desired, trim around outside of purse, sew fringe or other trim to right side of bag front and back. Place header of fringe along outside edge of bag front with bottom of fringe toward the center of the piece. If using multiple rows of fringe, place the first color of fringe along the edge as described and second color on top of first row. *Note: If using looped fringe, do not remove manufacturer's stabilizing thread along the bottom of the fringe until the fringe is stitched in place.*

2. (Optional) Arrange any embellishments you have chosen for the front and/or back that requires stitching on place on the right side and stitch. *Note: If embellishments are to be glued in place, wat until purse is completed.*

3. With right sides together, sew front piece to back piece, leaving top open. Turn and press. *Note: If you chose to trim around the purse, the fringe or trim will now be around the outside edge of sides and bottom of purse.*

4. With right sides together, sew front and back lining pieces together, leaving top open. Turn and press.

5. Slip lining into bag, wrong sides together. Sew with upper side edges together, leaving front and back tops open.

6. Turn under ½" at top of front and back, fold on fold line over first stitching line on lining. Sew through all layers. Press. Sew on second stitching line to form the channel for the purse rod, making a ruffle above the rod.

7. Unscrew caps off of one end of the two rods and insert them into the front and back channels, replace the caps.

8. Attach chain to purse frame.

9. Adhere remaining embellishments. See specific embellishment suggestions on the project page and the photograph of the bag you are making.

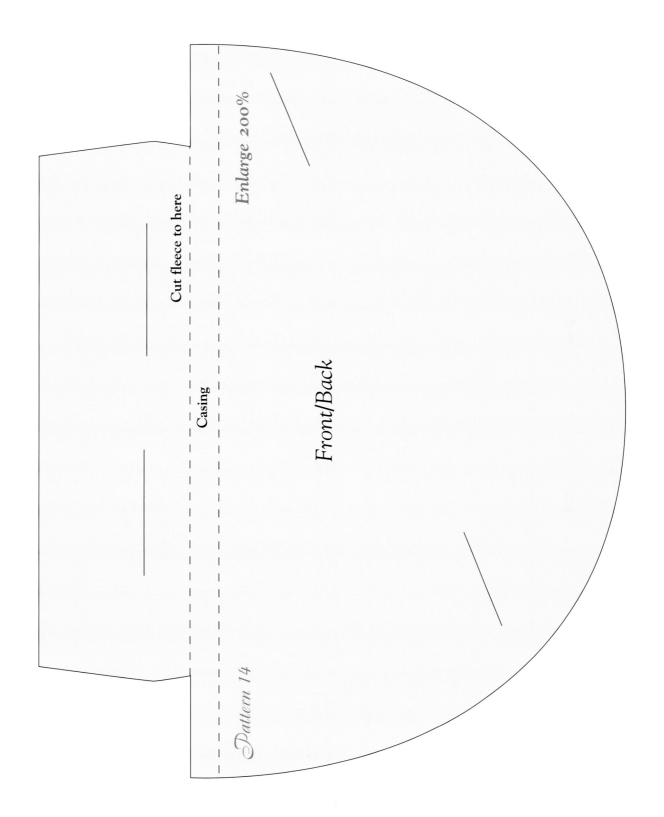

Cut fleece to here

Casing

Front/Back

Enlarge 200%

Pattern 14

Pattern 15

This pattern is used to construct the following purses:
Gypsy • Hearts & Flowers • Timeless Classic •
Wedding Party

Materials

- Embellishment for center of flower: chenille ball, fancy button, jewelry disk, or pin
- Eyelash fringe (15") for mum (optional)
- Felt circles, 2" dia. (2)
- Glues: fabric; industrial-strength
- Needle and thread
- Pin back
- Rayon looped fringe, ½"-wide (15")

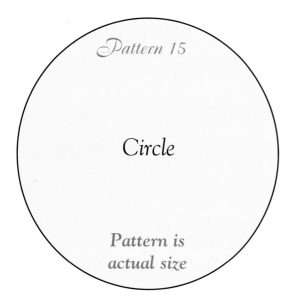

Pattern 15

Circle

*Pattern is
actual size*

Floppy Flower (6" diameter)

1. Starting in center of one felt circle, hand-stitch fringe to felt while coiling it three times, overlapping slightly at the end. Remove stabilizing thread from ends of petals and let them flop.

2. Sew or glue chosen item to the center of the blossom. If you have chosen a button, sew it in place securely and apply a little industrial strength glue under the button. If you have chosen a jewelry disk, glue it in place with the same strength glue. If you have chosen a chenille or boiled wool ball, use the fabric glue.

3. On second felt circle, put pinback hinges through small slits in the felt. Use a dab of strong glue under the pinback baron the under side of the felt circle. Adhere second circle to first circle with fabric glue.

Mum Blossom (4½" diameter)

1. (Optional) If adding eyelash fringe to blossom, sew header of fringe onto header of the looped fringe before you start.

2. Do not remove stabilizing thread from ends of looped fringe. Hand- or machine-stitch the stabilized end to the looped fringe header to make a double puffy fringe.

3. Starting in the center of one of the felt circles, hand-stitch the header of the fringe to the felt as you coil it around three times, overlapping slightly at the end.

4. Sew or glue item you have chosen for the center in place. If you have chosen a button, set it in place securely and apply a little industrial strength glue under the button. If you have chosen a jewelry disk, glue in lace with the same strong glue. If you have chosen a chenille or boiled wool ball, use fabric glue.

5. On the second felt circle, put the pinback hinges through small slits in the felt. Use a dab of strong glue under the bar of the pin back on the under side of the felt circle. Then, glue the second circle to the first circle with fabric glue.

Pattern 16

Finished size is 8" x 9½". Pattern assumes ½" seam allowances included in the pattern and seams are pressed open.

Materials

Note: This list is appropriate for a generic version of the pattern. See Materials and Embellishments lists that accompany the titled purse to make the specific design shown.

- Contrasting silk fabric, 6" x 12"
- Fusible fleece (⅓ yd)
- Glues: fabric; industrial-strength
- Narrow fancy trim to frame silk panel (1½ yds) (optional)
- Purse frame with handle
- Silk fabric (⅓ yd) for bag body
- Silk lining fabric (⅓ yd)

Preparation

1. Cut one one each of Front/Back pattern at right from basic fabric, lining fabric, and fleece.
2. Cut one piece of fleece to the size of the contrasting silk panel.
3. Fuse fleece to wrong side of basic fabric front and back pieces.
4. Fuse fleece to wrong side of silk panel.

Construction

1. Sew along bottom edge of front and back silk fabric pieces.
2. Appliqué silk panel to purse, wrapping around bottom edge of purse from front to back so that half is on the front and half is on the back.
3. Fold purse so right sides of front and back are together, sew side seams to marks on sides, leaving remainder of sides for purse frame.
4. If you have chosen to frame the silk panel, hand- or machine-stitch the narrow trim, add embellishing beads if desired.
5. With right sides together, sew lining front and back together, leaving top open. Press seams open.
6. Slip purse into the lining. With right sides together, sew side edges together and across top of front, leaving back open. Turn, press in open seams on the back, and sew close to the edge.
7. Hand-stitch purse through holes of purse frame. Stitch fabric on outside of frame and cover edge with trims, flowers, or beads.

Pattern 16

Front/Back

Enlarge 335%

Pattern 17

Finished size is 8" x 10" at widest point. Pattern assumes ½" seam allowances included in the pattern and seams are pressed open.

Materials

Note: This list is appropriate for a generic version of the pattern. See Materials and Embellishments lists that accompany the titled purse to make the specific design shown.

- Embroidered silk fabric (¼ yd) for body
- Fabric glue
- Flat scalloped trim (⅔ yd)
- Flower trim, ⅜"-wide (⅓ yd)
- Gold chain (40"–45")
- Gold metallic trim, ¼"–⅜"-wide (⅓ yd)
- Gold purse frame with holes, 4½"-wide
- Silk lining fabric (¼ yd)

Preparation

1. Cut one each of Front/Back pattern at right from basic fabric and lining fabric.

Construction

1. Sew scallop-edged trim to purse seam edge, starting at the mark on one side and sew around to the mark of the opposite side. Be certain to place the trim so the trim can be secured in the seams.

2. With right sides together, sew side and bottom seams to marks on sides, leaving top and upper sides above marks open for purse frame.

3. With right sides together, sew lining front and back to marks on sides, leaving top and upper sides above marks open.

4. Slip purse into lining. With right sides together, sew side seams together from marks and across top of front, leaving back open. Turn, press in raw edges of seams on the back, and sew close to the edge.

5. Hand-stitch the purse through the holes of the purse frame. Stitch the fabric on the outside of the frame and cover the edge with trims, flowers, or beads.

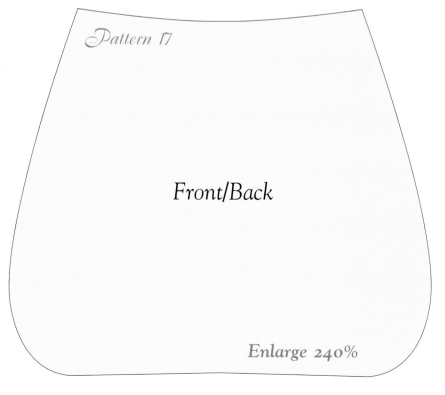

Pattern 17

Front/Back

Enlarge 240%

Pattern 18

Finished size is 8¼" sq.—not counting trim. Pattern assumes ½" seam allowances included in the pattern and seams are pressed open.

Materials

Note: This list is appropriate for a generic version of the pattern. See Materials and Embellishments lists that accompany the titled purse to make the specific design shown.

- Basic fabric, 45"-wide (⅓ yd)
- Fusible fleece (⅓ yd)
- Industrial-strength glue
- Purse frame with rods, 5½"-wide
- Silk lining fabric, 45"-wide (¼ yd)

Preparation

1. Cut two each of Front/Back pattern on page 136 from basic fabric and lining.
2. Cut two of Front/Back pattern to the first stitching line from fusible fleece.
3. Fuse fleece to wrong side of basic fabric pieces unless otherwise directed on design page.

Construction

1. For trims around outside of purse, sew fringe or other trim to right side of bag front and back. The header of the fringe should be placed long the outside edge of the bag front with the bottom of the fringe toward the venter of the piece. If you are using multiple rose of fringe, place the first color of fringe along the edge as described and second color on top of first row. *Note: If you are using looped fringe, do not remove the manufacturer's stabilizing thread along the bottom of the the fringe until the fringe is stitched in place.*

2. (Optional) Arrange any embellishments you have chosen or the front and /or back that requires stitching in place on the right side and stitch. *Note: If embellishments are to be glued, wait until the purse is completed.*

3. With right sides together, sew front and back basic fabric pieces together. Leave the top and upper sides open and turn and press. *Note: If you chose trim around the purse, the fringe or trim will now be around the outside edge of sides and bottom of purse.*

4. With right sides together, sew front and back lining pieces together, leaving the top and upper sides open. Turn and press.

5. With wrong sides together, slip lining into the bag. With upper side edges together, sew, leaving front and back tops open. Turn and press.

6. Turn under ½" at top of front and back, sew this folded edge to the first stitching line, sewing through all the layers. Sew on second stitching line to form the casing for the purse rod, making a ruffle above the rod.

7. Unscrew caps off of one end of a rod on purse frame front. Insert rod into ring on purse frame, insert into casing and then insert into ring on opposite side of the purse frame. Replace cap. Repeat on purse back.

8. Attach chain to purse frame.

9. Adhere remaining embellishments. See specific embellishment suggestions on the project page and the photograph of the bag you are making.

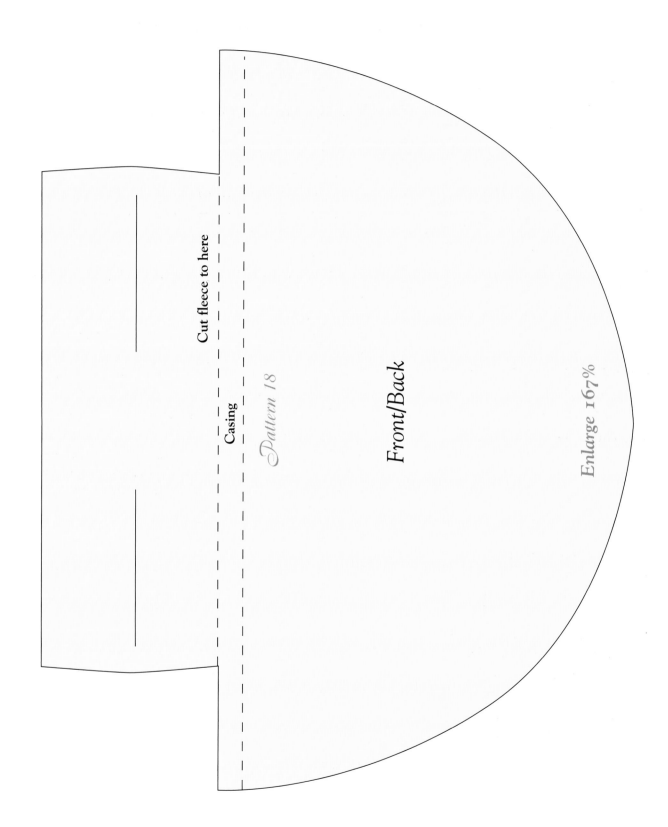

Cut fleece to here

Casing

Pattern 18

Front/Back

Enlarge 167%

Pattern 19

This pattern is used to construct the following purse:
Kismet

Finished size is 12" x 10½" x 4". Pattern assumes ½" seam allowances included in the pattern and seams are pressed open.

Materials

- Basic fabric (¾ yd) if no contrasting fabric used or (½ yd) if contrasting cuff fabric used
- Contrasting fabric (⅓ yd) for cuff (optional)
- Fringe, 2½"-wide (¾ yd) per row (optional)*
- Fusible fleece (⅓ yd)
- Fusible interfacing, 3"-wide strip
- Large buttons (2) (optional)
- Lining fabric (⅓ yd)
- Magnetic snaps

*Multiple rows of fringe or other trims add to the design. One dramatic corsage will add interest.

Preparation

1. Cut two of Front/Back pattern on page 138 from basic fabric.
2. Cut one of Cuff pattern on page 138 on fold.
3. Cut two each of Lining pattern at right from lining fabric and fleece.
4. Cut a 3" piece of interfacing to length of cuff piece.
5. Cut one of Strap pattern (3½" x 25") on page 138 from contrasting fabric.

Construction

1. With right sides together, sew front and back together along bottom edge and press seam open.
2. Sew side edges together and press seams open.
3. Bring side seams and bottom seam together, then sew across to form ends of purse bottom.
4. With right sides together, sew fringe around top of cuff in contrasting fabric. Set aside.
5. Sew back seam of cuff and press open.
6. Fuse 3" piece of fusible interfacing to inside of cuff, over the marks for the snaps.
7. With right sides together, sew cuff over flat trim and body. *Note: This will insert the trim into the seam.* Turn and press seam edge.
8. Following manufacturer's instructions, insert magnetic snaps on marks indicated on pattern.
9. Fuse fleece to lining and follow same method you used in making body of purse.
10. With right sides together, sew fleeced-lined lining to cuff, leaving about 8" open. Pull purse and lining to right side through opening. Push lining into purse. Hand-stitch opening securely with strong thread.

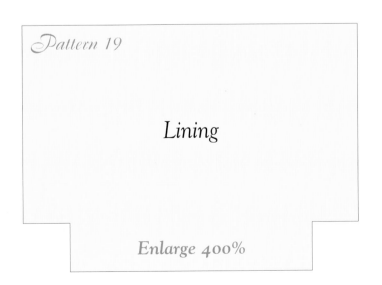

Pattern 19

Lining

Enlarge 400%

11. Select strap from the following methods:

Flat one fabric strap: Fold fabric in half lengthwise. Sew along the outside edge and press the seam open. *Note: If you stitch across one end of the strap, this makes turning easier and then you can snip this stitch end off after it is turned.* Turn and press flat with the seam in the center along the bottom of strap.

Flat fabric strap with suede cloth underside: Turn under 1" on both sides of fabric and on both sides of suede cloth and press. Place wrong sides together and edge-stitch with fabric on top and suede on bottom.

Flat fabric strap with trim: Fold the strap edges to the inside ¾" on each side, and press. Lay flat trim on top of the raw edges and sew to edges on each side of trim.

12. The strap can be sewn on side seams inside purse or on outside with buttons sewn and glued to cover stitching.

13. (Optional) Add corsage or other embellishments to cuff.

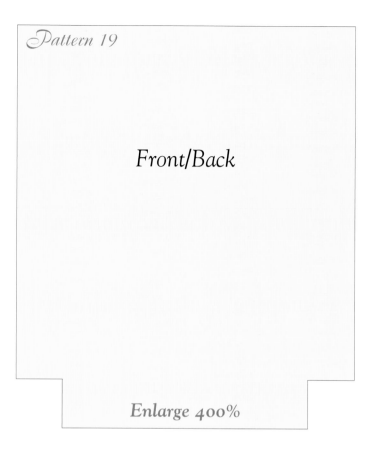

Pattern 19

Front/Back

Enlarge 400%

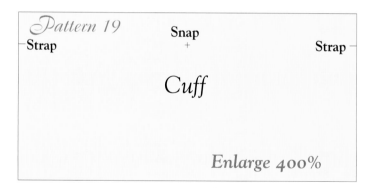

Pattern 19

Snap

Strap   Strap

Cuff

Enlarge 400%

Pattern 19

Strap

Enlarge 400%

Pattern 20

Finished size is 14" x 13" x 1¼"—not counting trim. Pattern assumes ½" seam allowances included in the pattern.

Materials

Note: This list is appropriate for a generic version of the pattern. See Materials and Embellishments lists that accompany the titled purse to make the specific design shown.

- Basic fabric (¾ yd)
- Contrasting fabric or grosgrain ribbon, 3½" x 72" for gusset and strap
- Fusible fleece (light or medium weight)** (⅔ yd)
- Fusible interfacing (⅓ yd)
- Lining fabric (⅔ yd)
- Looped fringe, ½"-wide (4⅛ yds)
- Magnetic snap
- Suede cloth, 3" x 30"

** Fusible fleece is not necessary if your basic fabric is heavy-weight.

Preparation

1. Cut one each of Front pattern on page 141 from basic fabric, lining fabric, and fusible fleece.

2. Cut one each of Back pattern on page 141 from basic fabric, lining fabric, and fusible fleece.

3. Cut one each of Flap pattern on poage 140 from basic fabric and fusible interfacing.

4. Cut one of Gusset pattern on page 141 from grosgrain ribbon or contrasting fabric.

5. Cut one each of Strap pattern (2½" x 30") on page 141 from contrasting fabric and suede cloth .

6. (Optional) Cut two pocket pieces from lining fabric.

Construction

1. Following manufacturer's directions, fuse fleece to wrong side of basic fabric front and back (fuse fleece to lining, if you prefer). Fuse interfacing to wrong side of flap. *Note: Use fleece in all silk and light or medium fabric purses. Use interfacing in the flaps and none in the body of heavier weight fabrics, unless otherwise stated in special patterns.*

2. (Optional) Sew two rows of looped fringe or other trim to right side of bag front. The fringe header should be placed along outside edge of bag front with bottom of fringe toward center of piece and sewn in place. Sew one row of looped fringe to outside edge of back of purse, using same method. *Note: Do not remove manufacturer's stabilizing thread along bottom of fringe until fringe is stitched in place.*

3. With right sides together, sew gusset to front. With right sides together, sew other side of gusset to back of purse, leaving top open. Tur.n. *Note: Fringe will now be around outside edge of sides and bottom of purse.*

4. (Optional) Arrange any embellishments you have chosen for the flap that require stitching in place on the right side of the flap and stitch. *Note: If embellishments are to be glued, wait until flap is completed. Sew fringe or trim around the flap using same method as purse body.*

5. Reinforce area on purse front and flap lining for magnetic snap with a 3" square of fused interfacing. Following manufacturer's instructions, attach magnetic snap, matching the "X" on purse front with bag flap. *Note: If using a regular snap, attach after purse is assembled.*

6. With right sides together, sew purse flap and flap lining together, leaving straight edge of flap open. Turn right side out and if you want a flat braid around flap, sew it in place around curved portion of flap. *Note: If this is too thick for your machine, stitch in place by hand after purse is assembled.*

7. Make the strap by pressing in 1" (or more for a narrow strap) on both sides of the fabric and folding in 1" (or more for a narrow strap) on both sides of the suede cloth. With wrong sides together, edge-stitch the fabric on top of the suede cloth. Place the strap ends on the side seams inside the bag, with outer side of strap facing right side of fabric and sew in place.

8. Center flap on back of bag and sew in place.

9. Slip bag inside lining, with right sides together. Sew around top of bag, leaving an opening for turning. Turn to right side, pushing lining into bag.

10. Turn in ½" seam of bag and lining and sew with either a slip-stitch or topstitch along edge.

11. Adhere remaining embellishments. See specific embellishment suggestions on the project page and the photograph of the bag you are making.

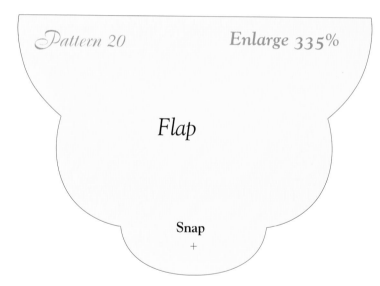

Pattern 20   Enlarge 335%

Flap

Snap

+

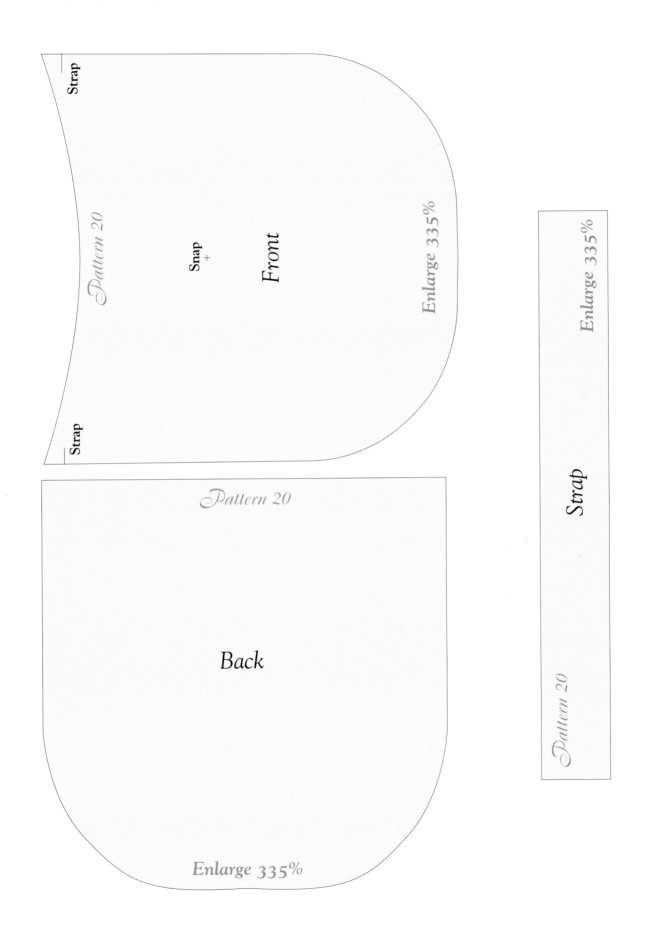

Strap

Pattern 20

Snap +

Front

Enlarge 335%

Strap

Strap

Pattern 20

Back

Enlarge 335%

Enlarge 335%

Strap

Pattern 20

About the Authors

Marilyn Green

Marilyn finds artistry in all she sees and this affects all she does. Having traveled widely as the wife of an army officer, she has learned not to see things in a conventional way. This has freed her from stifling rules and the "box" so many do not leave. The results are beautiful, unusual, even startling at times. She puts together lovely garments with the same enthusiasm as a delightful meal. She decorates her home in an interesting and unexpected style. It is such fun to be around this small dynamo and pick up some of the leftover energy and creativity.

She can be found in her studio that is brimming with fabrics and accouterments of every sort fresh from her collaborator in Ruby Tag Bags, Carole Cree and her online store Flights of Fancy Boutique. From this creative workplace come romantic purses with flair and fashion.

Marilyn's husband, Dale, is her port in a storm, when all about him seems crazy—he knows all is well. The Greens live in Fayetteville, Arkansas, where they met at the university and where, after years of the gypsy lifestyle, they returned to make a place for themselves and their daughter, Melissa.

Carole Cree

People like Carole are a breed unto themselves, having what I call the "eye." They are attracted to what others might see as mundane, seeing instead treasures of the past that can be used in the creation of beautiful, useful things. Carole has a reverence for these forgotten, surviving bits and pieces, and rescues them from molding in an attic or being discarded entirely. The term "old hat" takes on an entirely new meaning in this context. Even though Carole has boxes of lovely vintage pieces, she becomes enamored to each new find as if it were the first she has ever seen. There is an enthrallment hard to explain but easy to see in her satisfied smile and flashing green eyes.

The creations of this artisan, which have been sold at antique and quilt shows for years, need new materials as well as old and skills other than needle art. After searching for appropriate elements, she decided to form her own online company Flights of Fancy Boutique, the mother company of Ruby Tag Bags. In this way, the best of two worlds are brought together. Her collaboration with Marilyn Green is a bringing together of differing ideas and talents.

Carole lives in Fort Worth, Texas, with husband and right-hand man, Rick. They have three sons and two adorable grandsons.

Acknowledgments

Some of the most important words found in any book are those written with sincere gratitude to the behind-the-scenes people who make the book possible. This is especially true with this book. Without the fervent dedication, dogged determination, organizational skills, and unyielding spirit of Donna Brock, this book could not have happened. She kept us going when we were bogged down with the decision-making process, she supported us when we were unsure of our direction and she encouraged us when we thought we had surely lost our way. She waded through the tedious task of writing clear instructions and the endless maze of pattern designs and changes, eventually emerging with a finished product that in the end, finally made sense. We could, quite simply put, not have done it without her.

We are also grateful to our mutual friend Celeste Blackburn, who added her unique writing skills in describing each purse so eloquently. Thanks go to Susan Suggs for her one-of-a-kind floral creations using vintage millinery pieces, which form the spectacular centerpieces for several of the purses in our chapter Everything Old is New Again. We love the bas relief porcelain flapper lady from Helen Gibb, which adorns one of our favorite purses in the same chapter. We are always inspired by the extraordinary colors displayed in the fabrics, laces, and linens hand-dyed by our friend Wendy Richardson of Quilt Tapestry Studio. They provide a perfect backdrop for romantic purses and are featured in the chapter Delicate Enchantment. The online shop Flights of Fancy Boutique freely supplied many of the fabrics, trims, and embellishments used in this book—a blessing we feel we must acknowledge. To Mary Sue Evans who diligently maintains our Ruby Tag Bags Web site, we express our continuing gratitude.

And, we are blessed to have husbands whose love, support, and continued encouragement have enabled us to stay the course. So to Dale Green and Rick Cree—thank you!

Marilyn and Carole

Resources

Trims and embellishments used throughout this book were supplied by Flights of Fancy Boutique, www.flightsoffancyboutique.com.

The handbags shown in this book are available at Ruby Tag Bags, www.rubytagbags.com .

Pages 30–38
Custom-beaded button and beaded strap are originals by Judy Hendrix. This wonderful collection can be seen in a boutique at www.flightsoffancyboutique.com.

Pages 72, 80, 84, 86
Vintage and designer brooches and corsages by Susan Suggs.

Pages 86–87
'Nola' flapper bas relief is an original by Helen Gibb and is available on her Web site, www.helengibb.com.

Pages 63–64
Overdyed fabrics and trims by Wendy Richardson, www.qtstudio.com.

Index

Metric Conversions

inches to millimeters and centimeters							yards to meters									
inches	mm	cm	inches	cm	inches	cm	yards	meters	yards	meters	yards	meters	yards	meters	yards	meters
⅛	3	0.3	9	22.9	30	76.2	⅛	0.11	2⅛	1.94	4⅛	3.77	6⅛	5.60	8⅛	7.43
¼	6	0.6	10	25.4	31	78.7	⅛	0.11	2⅛	1.94	4⅛	3.77	6⅛	5.60	8⅛	7.43
½	13	1.3	12	30.5	33	83.8	¼	0.23	2¼	2.06	4¼	3.89	6¼	5.72	8¼	7.54
⅝	16	1.6	13	33.0	34	86.4	⅜	0.34	2⅜	2.17	4⅜	4.00	6⅜	5.83	8⅜	7.66
¾	19	1.9	14	35.6	35	88.9	½	0.46	2½	2.29	4½	4.11	6½	5.94	8½	7.77
⅞	22	2.2	15	38.1	36	91.4	⅝	0.57	2⅝	2.40	4⅝	4.23	6⅝	6.06	8⅝	7.89
1	25	2.5	16	40.6	37	94.0	¾	0.69	2¾	2.51	4¾	4.34	6¾	6.17	8¾	8.00
1¼	32	3.2	17	43.2	38	96.5	⅞	0.80	2⅞	2.63	4⅞	4.46	6⅞	6.29	8⅞	8.12
1½	38	3.8	18	45.7	39	99.1	1	0.91	3	2.74	5	4.57	7	6.40	9	8.23
1¾	44	4.4	19	48.3	40	101.6	1⅛	1.03	3⅛	2.86	5⅛	4.69	7⅛	6.52	9⅛	8.34
2	51	5.1	20	50.8	41	104.1	1¼	1.14	3¼	2.97	5¼	4.80	7¼	6.63	9¼	8.46
2½	64	6.4	21	53.3	42	106.7	1⅜	1.26	3⅜	3.09	5⅜	4.91	7⅜	6.74	9⅜	8.57
3	76	7.6	22	55.9	43	109.2	1½	1.37	3½	3.20	5½	5.03	7½	6.86	9½	8.69
3½	89	8.9	23	58.4	44	111.8	1⅝	1.49	3⅝	3.31	5⅝	5.14	7⅝	6.97	9⅝	8.80
4	102	10.2	24	61.0	45	114.3	1¾	1.60	3¾	3.43	5¾	5.26	7¾	7.09	9¾	8.92
4½	114	11.4	25	63.5	46	116.8	1⅞	1.71	3⅞	3.54	5⅞	5.37	7⅞	7.20	9⅞	9.03
5	127	12.7	26	66.0	47	119.4	2	1.83	4	3.66	6	5.49	8	7.32	10	9.14
6	152	15.2	27	68.6	48	121.9										
7	178	17.8	28	71.1	49	124.5										
8	203	20.3	29	73.7	50	127.0										